THE TECH SET

Ellyssa Kroski, Series Editor

Semantic Web Technologies and Social Searching for Librarians

Robin M. Fay and Michael P. Sauers

ALA TechSource

An imprint of the American Library Association

Chicago   2012

Printed in the United States of America

Library of Congress Cataloging-in-Publication Data
Fay, Robin M.
  Semantic Web technologies and social searching for librarians / Robin M. Fay, Michael P. Sauers.
      p. cm. — (The tech set ; #20)
  Includes bibliographical references and index.
  ISBN 978-1-55570-780-4 (alk. paper)
  1. Semantic Web. 2. Libraries and the Internet. 3. Libraries—Information technology. 4. Metadata. 5. Social media. I. Sauers, Michael P. II. Title.

ZA4240.F39 2012
025.04'27—dc23

                                                                    2012007205

⊚ This paper meets the requirements of ANSI/NISO Z39.48-1992 (Permanence of Paper).

CONTENTS

Don't miss this book's companion website!

Turn the page for details.

THE TECH SET® Volumes 11–20 is more than just the book you're holding!

These 10 titles, along with the 10 titles that preceded them, in THE TECH SET® series feature three components:

1. This book
2. Companion web content that provides more details on the topic and keeps you current
3. Author podcasts that will extend your knowledge and give you insight into the author's experience

The companion webpages and podcasts can be found at:

www.alatechsource.org/techset/

On the website, you'll go far beyond the printed pages you're holding and:

- ▸ Access author updates that are packed with new advice and recommended resources
- ▸ Use the website comments section to interact, ask questions, and share advice with the authors and your LIS peers
- ▸ Hear these pros in screencasts, podcasts, and other videos providing great instruction on getting the most out of the latest library technologies

For more information on THE TECH SET® series and the individual titles, visit **www.neal-schuman.com/techset-11-to-20**.

FOREWORD

New trends in search technology are competing to meet our information retrieval needs. Today's search tools are making use of structured and linked data, real-time search techniques, and social search. *Semantic Web Technologies and Social Searching for Librarians* is a comprehensive guide that outlines everything from semantic search to data visualizations to how to track and start trends. Authors Robin Fay and Michael Sauers explain the principles behind the Semantic Web, how you can structure your own data for better retrieval by today's semantic search engines, and the secrets of finding hidden content online. Packed with projects such as how to semanticize your data with Google's Rich Snippets to exploring data and statistics through WolframAlpha, to tracking your library's reputation through social search, this all-in-one handbook delivers invaluable instructions for cutting-edge search and Semantic Web initiatives in your library.

The ten new TECH SET volumes are designed to be even more cutting-edge than the original ten. After the first ten were published and we received such positive feedback from librarians who were using the books to implement technology in their libraries as well as train their staff, it seemed that there would be a need for another TECH SET. And I wanted this next set of books to be even more forward-looking and tackle today's hottest technologies, trends, and practices to help libraries stay on the forefront of technology innovation. Librarians have ceased sitting on the sidelines and have become technology leaders in their own right. This series was created to offer guidance and inspiration to all those aspiring to be library technology leaders themselves.

I originally envisioned a series of books that would offer accessible, practical information that would teach librarians not only how to use new technologies as individuals but also how to plan and implement particular types of library services using them. And when THE TECH SET won the ALA's Greenwood Publishing Group Award for the Best Book in Library Literature, it seemed that we had achieved our goal of becoming the go-to resource for libraries wanting hands-on technology primers. For these new ten books, I thought it was important to incorporate reader feedback by adding two new chapters to each volume that would better facilitate learning how to put these new technologies into practice in libraries. The new chapter called "Social Mechanics" discusses strategies for gaining buy-in and support from organizational stakeholders, and the additional "Developing Trends" chapter looks ahead to future directions of these technologies. These new chapters round out the books that discuss the entire life cycle of these tech initiatives, including everything from what it takes to plan, strategize, implement, market, and measure the success of these projects.

While each book covers the A–Zs of each technology being discussed, the hands-on "Implementation" chapters, chock-full of detailed project instructions, account for the largest portions of the books. These chapters start off with a basic "recipe" for how to effectively use the technology in a library and then build on that foundation to offer more and more advanced project ideas. Because these books are designed to appeal to readers of all levels of expertise, both the novice and advanced technologist will find something useful in these chapters, as the proposed projects and initiatives run the gamut from the basic how to create a Foursquare campaign for your library to how to build an iPhone application. Similarly, the new Drupal webmaster will benefit from the instructions for how to configure a basic library website, while the advanced web services librarian may be interested in the instructions for powering a dynamic library website in the cloud using Amazon's EC2 service.

Robin Fay and Michael Sauers have both been writing and speaking about web technology in libraries for many years. These two authorities on search and the Semantic Web teamed up to put together an exceptional book with *Semantic Web Technologies and Social Searching for Librarians*. If you're seeking to learn all there is to know about cutting-edge search tools and semantic technologies, this is a must-read resource.

Ellyssa Kroski
Manager of Information Systems
New York Law Institute
http://www.ellyssakroski.com/
http://oedb.org/blogs/ilibrarian/
ellyssakroski@yahoo.com

Ellyssa Kroski is the Manager of Information Systems at the New York Law Institute as well as a writer, educator, and international conference speaker. In 2011, she won the ALA's Greenwood Publishing Group Award for the Best Book in Library Literature for THE TECH SET, the ten-book technology series that she created and edited. She's also the author of *Web 2.0 for Librarians and Information Professionals*, a well-reviewed book on web technologies and libraries. She speaks at several conferences a year, mainly about new tech trends, digital strategy, and libraries. She is an adjunct faculty member at Pratt Institute and blogs at *iLibrarian*.

PREFACE

Technology changes every day, and the web continues to evolve. We are not suddenly going to wake up and discover a different web; it will slowly become more personalized and more customizable. Computers and other machines will be able to help us make decisions and sort information more accurately. The web is also becoming smarter as developers use semantics to structure data for better retrieval by today's search engines. *Semantic Web Technologies and Social Searching for Librarians* will help you understand these techniques and thus how to both use them in your own library's website and uncover the secrets of finding hidden content.

Web technology changes are facilitated by the sheer volume of data that is collected about us, about our world, and about our resources data that we share, organize, tag, post, and share. According to the Digital Universe Study (EMC2's Digital Universe, http://www.emc.com/leadership/programs/digital-universe.htm), 1.8 zettabytes of information will be created and replicated in 2011—that's 1.8 trillion gigabytes! This wealth of data and the ability of computers and other electronics to be smarter means that our mobile devices can give us real-time information about which books are available in our library or which events are happening that day, what the weather will be should we want to walk to the library (and give us walking directions), or, should we change our mind about walking, real-time traffic and parking info. We can read reviews of books on mobile devices and add our reviews, too. All of this information is driven by behind-the-scenes data. We (and our patrons) are increasingly dealing with this vast quantity of information, at times making it harder to find what is really important. This puts libraries in an even more critical role as content curators and content brokers.

We designed *Semantic Web Technologies and Social Searching for Librarians* to help librarians and information professionals learn new skills, programs, and technologies that will help them stay current with technological evolution instead of continuously scrambling to catch up. Our patrons expect us to be technology experts. This means that we need to be able to both use and search the technology effectively. New trends in search technology are competing to meet our information retrieval needs. Today, search tools are making use of structured and linked data, real-time search techniques, and social search.

▶ AUDIENCE AND ORGANIZATION

Semantic Web Technologies and Social Searching for Librarians is designed to be a practical guide for all librarians wanting to learn about the future of web-based technology, especially those interested in search. Managers, those working in the technology side of libraries, as well as those who assist patrons in researching material in the library catalog and other databases will benefit greatly from this book. Chapter 1 introduces the fundamentals of social search, the Semantic Web, and metadata. Chapter 2 explores semantic technology as well as the type of search available: location based, maps, local, real time, visualizations, multimedia, social, and semantic. Chapter 3 looks to the real library projects for inspiration and provides tips on planning technology projects. Chapter 4 focuses on social mechanics, the human element of planning technology projects: committees, meetings, and getting buy-in. Chapter 5's step-by-step guide through practical projects is divided between search and Semantic Web projects. Projects for this chapter were carefully selected with an eye toward stability. Given the ever-changing world of new technologies, with new products popping up and disappearing at an astounding rate, projects in Chapter 5 are fully developed while still being on the edge of new technologies. Chapter 6 provides tips on marketing for technology projects; Chapter 7 provides some best practices; and Chapter 8 focuses on metrics and measures of success. Rounding out the book is a discussion of future trends and a recommended reading list.

Semantic Web Technologies and Social Searching for Librarians provides library and information professionals with the knowledge and skills necessary to implement Semantic Web technology; additionally, the search projects are crucial to those looking to hone their searching and research skills. There is a wealth of new tools for the searcher's toolbox, and this book tackles them. The Semantic Web is not brand-new. Some of the technologies explored in *Semantic Web Technologies and Social Searching for Librarians* you have probably heard of and may already be using. If you are using them, you most likely had no idea of how they worked. Understanding more about how they will work will make you a better searcher and researcher—one of the strongest tools a searcher can have. The future of the web is semantic, and the future is here.

ACKNOWLEDGMENTS

Robin:

Thank you to all of the people who have inspired and helped me along the way. May you continue to innovate, grow, and create. My biggest thanks to Ellyssa and Michael.

Michael:

Many thanks to Emily Nimsakont (for help with RDA), Karen Coyle (for offering introductions), Jon Voss (for helping out in a crunch), and Ellyssa (for bringing me in on this project). It's been quite an experience.

▶1

INTRODUCTION

- ▶ What You Will Learn
- ▶ What a Semantic Search Is
- ▶ What the Semantic Web Is
- ▶ How It All Works

The Semantic Web. The Social Web. Social search. Metadata. Linked data. To most people these words have little meaning despite the importance of what they are and what they will become. Tired of wading through millions of search results looking for the "right" thing? Think that there must be a "better" way to find things for both you and your patrons?

Search engines return millions of results, which no group of searchers of any size, never mind one person, can possibly view and evaluate. Social media sites expand the concept of friends to anyone you wish to add to your online network, increasing your ability to get advice, learn, network, find others for social media gaming, and, yes, even find life partners. Social search is leveraging the collective knowledge of the world to find what you need. Social search encompasses both the Social Web and what exists of the Semantic Web today.

This practical primer will focus on leveraging new search and Semantic Web tools to create better user experiences. It will provide the steps that those who create data and websites can take to make your library's resources both more accessible on today's web and ready for the future. The projects we provide all include ideas that you can put into place now and encompass both the Social Web and the Semantic Web. They are easy to implement and require only minimal technical know-how.

▶ WHAT YOU WILL LEARN

We set out with several goals for this book. By the time you're done reading it, you should:

1. have better ways to find what you are looking for, tapping into the newest and most innovative search strategies, including mining social media and hidden content across the web;
2. have a solid understanding of the concepts of the Semantic Web and understand why it is important to the next stages in the evolution of online resources; and
3. be knowledgeable about practical applications for the Semantic Web and have tools you can use to align your resources for the Semantic Web of the future.

► WHAT A SEMANTIC SEARCH IS

A semantic search is a new way of searching that takes advantage of connecting data. In many cases, for a semantic search to work, the underlying concepts of the Semantic Web must first be in place. Some of them, such as location-based data, are already in wide use, while others, such as microformats (covered in Chapter 5), are still in the early stages of implementation. A few examples of new semantic search technologies include location-based searching (Bing Maps), real-time searching (Twitter's Real Time Search), and social searching, such as Google's Social Search features, which are still listed as "experimental."

► WHAT THE SEMANTIC WEB IS

The notion of the Semantic Web has been around at least since 2001, but the notion of the evolving web has been around much longer. The concept involves us adding context to our data so that computers can do more of the work for us.

The Semantic Web is customizable and personalizable; it provides a better means of filtering your search results and relies on the idea that giving context to data makes that data more rich and the searches "smarter." The Semantic Web relies on metadata and linking data together (linked data) and encompasses a variety of formats, such as images and video. Another feature of the Semantic Web is the ability to weave social media (blogs, Twitter feeds, tumblogs, etc.) into search results. This next stage of connecting and inter-connecting data on the web is the Semantic Web. Being able to search that content and to take advantage of all those connections is semantic search. The Semantic Web is not a radical change but an evolution. Additionally, it is not solely data driven, as much of the metadata is created by users through practices such as tagging.

We are not suddenly going to wake up one day to find that all of the resources in the world have been made available via the Semantic Web.

Considering many resources are still in analog formats, there is a lot of work to be done before much of that content is converted to a digital format, let alone have good metadata and linked data associated with it. Even more work is needed before everything has metadata in a form that can be used by search engines. However, we are already seeing Semantic Web features and functionalities showing up in online search tools and even in some library catalogs. With these features we can better customize our searches for our specific needs. We can interact with data in new ways, whether through tagging library catalog records or creating reading lists.

Much of the data generated by libraries, museums, and other information-based institutions is siloed. In other words, each kind or group of data sits in its own container (typically a database), often with a proprietary structure around it, making it nearly impossible to be searched via a web-based search engine. One of the biggest examples of this kind of data is the library catalog; in some cases records can be harvested by search engines, but even then they are extraordinarily hard to find.

As libraries move toward new standards and rules for creating semantic library catalog metadata records, specifically FRBR (http://www.ifla.org/en/publications/functional-requirements-for-bibliographic-records) and the forthcoming RDA (http://www.rdatoolkit.org/) (discussed later in this chapter), there is much hope that this information will become less invisible to the web. Knowing more about the Semantic Web means that librarians will understand why their data works (or doesn't) with search engines. The goal of the Semantic Web is to take all of the "stuff" on the web, including library content, and put it together in a way that is accessible and usable to the general public and to provide a better means of filtering and controlling that information.

Of course, there is more to the web than just searching; the Semantic Web will allow even more leveraging of mobile devices. For example, a typical smartphone today allows you to search for a restaurant based on your current location, sort the results by best review and/or distance, book a reservation for you (assuming the restaurant has an online presence), provide directions (driving or walking), and send all of that information to your friends all in a matter of minutes. In the not-so-distant past, this scenario would have seemed like science fiction, but it is a reality today. The ability to do these kinds of things using a mobile device is based on data and the ability of the device to communicate with the web. Bits of data and the relationships among them (e.g., reviews linked to a restaurant's website) are examples of how the Semantic Web can (and does!) work.

Another example of the Semantic Web is Amazon.com's recommendation service. Using semantic markup and semantic search, Amazon analyzes what you've looked at and/or ordered and makes a recommendation. Providing more relevant results for your search is a big part of the Semantic Web, but it goes beyond that. It is facilitating the dialogue between devices and people, making our lives easier. In the future, your "smart" refrigerator may keep an inventory of its contents and add items to your shopping list that you are low on. Then, when you're driving home, your phone will alert you to the fact that you need to stop to pick up more milk. You and your friends or colleagues might collaborate on a novel online, publish it automatically to a variety of sources, and automatically link reviews to it. The Semantic Web doesn't care about where the data comes from.

Wow, is there a lot of stuff to wade through on the web! Images, podcasts, statistical data, websites, documents, maps, blog posts; the list is practically endless. How can we possibly find what we really need? If the goal of the Semantic Web is to take all of the "stuff" on the web and pull it together in a way that is usable, how does this happen? What makes it work? Do you need to know how it works in order to use it? Ultimately, the hope is that the answer to that last question becomes "no." However, given that the Semantic Web and semantic search are still developing, knowing more about how they work behind the scenes may save a headache or two down the road when trying to decide what kinds of projects to do or even how to do them. Knowing a little bit about how they work means that you can better use the resources that exist and explain them to friends, patrons, a child who needs homework help, and others. You will be more information literate.

▶ HOW IT ALL WORKS

Metadata is the key to the Semantic Web. It is like a translation service, allowing programs to talk to each other and "understand" the data they find. "Metadata" is a scary word to a lot of people; it conjures up confusion with its definition of "data about data." True, this is what metadata *is*, but it doesn't really tell us what metadata *does* or how we can use it. We already have machines that talk to the web—desktops, laptops, netbooks, MP3 players, streaming television devices, tablets, e-readers, phones, even cars and cameras. Metadata is simply the language used to communicate among devices, databases, items, and objects.

How about a real-life example of metadata? Let's consider my dog. When I got a new dog, one of the first questions people asked is what kind of dog is it. My dog is an Australian shepherd. Other questions were how old is it, its name, and its gender. Each feature about the dog can be thought of in terms of metadata. These features are bits of descriptive metadata, because they describe the dog. My dog is a five-year-old female Australian Shepherd named Roxy. All of these features are coded into a database at my vet's office, and this database could share those bits of metadata, even with another vet's office. Going further into the metadata analogy, my dog is assigned an ID number, which is a unique number, a **unique resource identifier**. On the practical side of things, this keeps all of her information together and ensures that her medical history is not mixed up with another dog's. From a metadata standpoint, she has a metadata record with a unique number.

Libraries have been creating metadata for a very long time, although traditionally the largest focus has been on descriptive metadata. Descriptive metadata describes what an item is, with a goal of identifying the object and making it findable. This type of metadata is the foundation of library catalog records. Looking at the catalog record of a book, its title, author's name, notes, and subject headings are all descriptive information. There are three major types of metadata (see Figure 1.1):

1. Descriptive
2. Structural
3. Administrative

▶ Figure 1.1: Types of Metadata

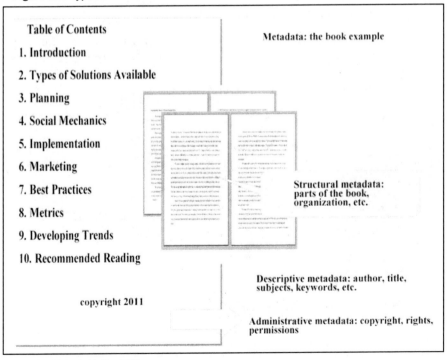

Source: Graphic by Robin Fay, 2011.

Different communities organize metadata into different groupings; however, all metadata depend on a schema, a set of rules for the elements and attributes, and the rules for how that information should be arranged. Descriptive metadata describes the item itself, using titles and topic description (keywords, subject headings, and tags). Structural metadata explains the nature of the object, such as how many parts are included in the overall object. In a book, for example, this might be the pages, how the pages form chapters, or format. Administrative metadata includes information about how to handle or process the object. In the example of Roxy's vet record, administrative metadata might include her owner's information; for a letter or painting, it might include the chain of ownership (i.e., the provenance). One of the most commonly used types of administrative metadata on the web is ownership rights metadata. One format that many are familiar with these days is Digital Rights Management (DRM), the licensing that allows the use of commercially produced digital files, such as music, movies, and e-books.

Let's take a look at a common type of audio file, .mp3. These files generally have a variety of metadata associated with them (see Figure 1.2):

- ► Title > Descriptive
- ► Song no./album info > Structural
- ► Licensing/limits > Administrative/rights

Metadata is the data that describes an object (photo, book, your dog, etc.) in a database (such as your vet's patient database; to an even larger

► Figure 1.2: Metadata on an MP3 Player Display

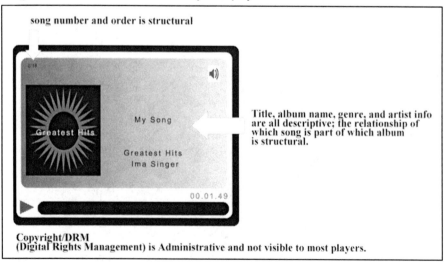

Source: Graphic by Robin Fay, 2011.

extent, the World Wide Web), explains how to display it, and who has access to it.

How do creators of metadata know how or where to add it? Users at social sites such as Facebook, Flickr, and YouTube create metadata through a guided system. By typing in the title of a video or photo, the user is creating descriptive metadata. Some metadata can actually be embedded into the file itself by the device that creates it. For example, many digital cameras now record the type of camera and the file format into the file itself. When a user uploads a photo file to Flickr, Flickr will recognize it as a .jpg format and often will be able to retrieve (harvest) the camera make and model from the file itself. In both cases, the metadata that is created follows instructions for displaying the information, as determined by its schema (rules). We'll look into this example further in Chapter 5.

Linked Data

In the Semantic Web world there is no limit to number and diversity of schemas as long as there is some way (usually through a link pointing back to the schema file) for a search engine or other semantic tool to access the schema. Just making all of the data in the world accessible doesn't necessarily create a way for people to find it.

The web has always allowed us to create links between webpages and files, and that's a great first step. When we add a link to a webpage, post a link to Facebook or Twitter, or embed a video in a blog post, we have created a link from one resource to another. However, that link has no context other than what we provide with it. For example, users can only assume that a link that reads "White House" will lead them to the White House's website. The contexts of links are created manually by site content editors, and we need to trust them to actually link us to the content they've implied they're taking us to.

The Semantic Web uses linked data to do just what its name implies—link individual items of data together, creating points of connection, relationships, and/or context so that we can find what we're searching for. Linked data is created by computers based on data, instead of just a link (or links) to files, that we create when we link to a website. For example, recommendation services ("If you bought this, you might like this...") rely on creating a connection between like items to make that recommendation.

RDA

Resource Description and Access (RDA) is a new code of cataloging rules, designed to replace the *Anglo-American Cataloguing Rules*, Second Edition (AACR2), as the law of the cataloging land. RDA was released by the Joint

Steering Committee for Development of RDA in June 2010, and the rules were subsequently evaluated in a testing process by three U.S. national libraries (the Library of Congress, the National Library of Medicine, and the National Agricultural Library). The result of the test was the decision that RDA will be adopted but no earlier than January 2013. Even though it has not been officially implemented yet, RDA has the potential to greatly change library data and how that data interacts with other information on the web.

What can RDA do for your library data, and how can it help libraries get ready for the Semantic Web? For one thing, RDA has the potential to break library records down into smaller pieces of information, some of which can be provided in a machine-actionable format. Right now, bibliographic description according to AACR2 is based on eight areas of description. For example, one area of description deals with information relating to the publication of the item being cataloged, and, in a catalog record, this area in AACR2 could look like this: Chicago, Ill. : American Library Association, c2011. A number of different pieces of information are expressed in this one area: place of publication, publisher, and copyright date. In RDA, each of these three smaller pieces of information is its own element.

RDA also clarifies how different types of information should be recorded within an area. To return to the example of publication information, some AACR2 records have publication dates: Chicago, Ill. : American Library Association, 2011. Others have copyright dates: Chicago, Ill. : American Library Association, c2011. Right now, the presence of the letter "c" before the date is the only thing that indicates to the human reader that the date is a copyright date and not a publication date, and there is no way at all for a computer to understand the difference between these dates. According to RDA, publication date and copyright date are two different elements. Because it explicitly indicates particular elements for specific pieces of information, RDA is the first step toward creating data that can be recognized by computers as particular types of information and therefore integrated into Semantic Web searches.

In addition to breaking down catalog records into smaller pieces of data, RDA also specifies a great deal more data to be included in authority records to represent the creators of the items in library catalogs. New authority elements include occupation, gender, and associated places, and authority records created according to RDA are much richer sources of information than the ones currently used. This is a good thing, because the more information that libraries have, the more opportunities they have to link their data to other sources in the Semantic Web.

A third change that RDA will bring to cataloging is an emphasis on the relationships between pieces of data in catalog records and between catalog records for different items. RDA's rules are based on a conceptual model called the *Functional Requirements for Bibliographic Records*, or FRBR. FRBR identifies the entities that are represented in library catalogs and their relationships to each other, as well as their relationships to the creators of these entities and the subjects of these entities.

To understand the effects of FRBR on library catalogs, think about searching for an item like *Romeo and Juliet*. When searching a so-called "FRBR-ized" catalog for *Romeo and Juliet*, patrons would be able to find all of the various editions of that work in an easily navigable display rather than having to view different records for each edition. In addition, catalog users could find movie adaptations of the play and even related works, such as *West Side Story*.

The changes introduced by RDA and FRBR could have a great effect on libraries, even within the confines of their own catalogs. However, the real power of RDA is its potential to integrate library information with other information on the web. If library records are broken down into pieces of data, the principles of linked data can be used to create connections to other sources of information on the web. If this happens, it will be possible to retrieve library data through searches that do not start with the library's catalog. A search like the one for *Romeo and Juliet* could result in information from a number of sources being brought together without having to search the sources independently.

RDA is the library profession's way of preparing metadata to be ready for use by Semantic Web search engines; other information communities are developing their own ways to prepare metadata for their materials so that they can be harvested. Libraries have exciting times ahead—ready to get started?

▶ 2

TYPES OF SOLUTIONS AVAILABLE

- ▶ Use Location-Based Searching
- ▶ Use Real-Time Searching
- ▶ Use Visualization for Searching
- ▶ Use Multimedia Searching
- ▶ Use Social Searching
- ▶ Use Semantic Searching

In this chapter, we will explore types of Semantic Web and search tools currently available. Semantic search involves harnessing the power of the Semantic Web, giving libraries the necessary tools to provide better and more tailored services to our users, in addition to laying a foundation for understanding the new technologies driving our websites and products. We'll focus on real-life examples of location-based search, social search, data search, search visualization, and media search.

▶ USE LOCATION-BASED SEARCHING

Emerging trends in location-based search include using a combination of a mobile device and GPS and/or WiFi services to tailor localized information to the searcher. Mobile devices connect the user to a range of services and applications; these applications generally ask the user for permission to include location-related information in searching so that results can be oriented around the individual's location. Another example of location-based searching is up-to-the-minute traffic reports, some even showing accidents or real-time video footage from traffic cameras.

Although there may not be a direct need for such services at a traditional reference desk, for several reasons librarians should be familiar with these services. First, even though reference librarians may not use the services themselves, it is likely they will be asked about how one works. Reference librarians need to be able to answer such questions. Second, more and more reference services are being supplied by libraries not at traditional reference desks. For example, we've heard of librarians who take a laptop to the student union or the local coffee shop and set up an ad hoc mobile reference desk. In such cases, being able to help people find directions from locations other than the library could come in quite handy.

Maps and Local Searches

Both Google and Bing provide a "local" search, showing you restaurants, businesses, and other points of interest, which are then displayed geographically in association with their respective mapping services. However, focusing your search starting with their mapping services provides many other possibilities.

For example, when using Google Maps (http://maps.google.com/) you can click on the "Traffic" option, which will not only provide an overlay displaying major roads but also note traffic problems (as green, yellow, or red). Additionally, you can search "Live Traffic" or limit the search to a particular time period, in effect retrieving a snapshot history of traffic for a particular area based on past traffic problems. This ability to obtain historical traffic information can be helpful when navigating a new city. For example, you need to get to the airport but have no idea how long the drive will take; seeing past traffic history for the time and day of the week can help in planning. Google Maps also includes transit and walking directions, as well as the ability to search for places nearby.

Bing Maps (http://www.bing.com/maps/) predominantly features traffic, highlighting traffic cameras and current traffic (see Figure 2.1). Bing Maps also shows directions, including transit and walking maps as well as links to Map apps for taxi fare calculators and gas prices.

Social Media

Social media also offers location-based searching. Twitter allows searching by location, and both Gowalla (http://gowalla.com/) and Foursquare (http://www.foursquare.com/) are at their core location based. Besides offering the ability to search for a business based on the user's current location, both Gowalla and Foursquare operate as a kind of social media game. Using their mobile devices, users can check in at a location to both earn points and collect badges (Foursquare) or stamps (Gowalla) that show that they've performed some task (e.g., voted in an election) or regularly appeared at a certain type of venue (e.g., checked in at a number of Starbucks to earn the Barista badge). In Foursquare players can also become the "mayor" of a location by checking in more often than all other players.

▷ Figure 2.1: Bing Map for Boston Public Library

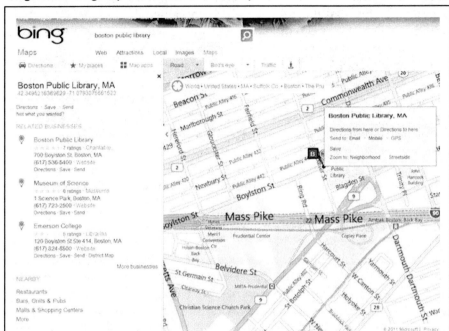

Not all geographic-based sites and services are new; GPS and geocaching (a GPS-related scavenger hunt) have been around for a while (http://www .geocaching.com/). Such sites rely on GPS to interact with mobile devices and to capture real-time information from traffic cameras and other traffic sensors.

▷ USE REAL-TIME SEARCHING

Sometimes you'd like to do a search of online content to see what is being said about a topic *right now.* In other words, you'd like information as it occurs in real time. This is where the concept of real-time searching comes into play—when you want to see new results as they are posted to the web. Real-time searching provides a window into current events, breaking news, and what people are talking about on social media networks.

For example, Bing displays real-time searches from Twitter as the results update within the Bing Social (http://www.bing.com/social/) search. Bing Social displays real-time results of both tweets and links that people have shared on Twitter. This option displays results with the newest at the top and tells how long it has been since the website or post was updated. (The time stamps for websites do not indicate the time something was posted about the search topic, just that the webpage which contained the topic was updated.) Additionally, the page will update itself, adding new results as they happen. (We'll talk about this a lot more in Chapter 5.)

Real-time search is still in its infancy, but a number of new services (e.g., Social Mention, http://www.socialmention.com/; Collecta, http://collecta .com/; and Topsy, http://topsy.com/) are already trying to become front-runners in real-time searching. Most services, including Microsoft's Bing Social, focus specifically on social sources. Given the potential that the Internet has to get information from an event out to the world quickly, real-time searching is particularly effective in identifying trending topics (including what people are saying about your library) and finding breaking news.

▶ USE VISUALIZATION FOR SEARCHING

A visualization is a graphical representation of information. Examples include traditional images such as pie charts and bar graphs as well as infographics such as mind maps, timelines, and network diagrams. All of these can be useful when attempting to understand data but can also be used to represent social networks, relationships, and more. Let's take a look at two examples: WolframAlpha and Google News Timeline.

WolframAlpha and Data Visualization

WolframAlpha (http://www.wolframalpha.com/) bills itself as a "computational knowledge engine," and at its heart it's a semantic search engine focused on statistical information and data sets. It supports natural language query and real-time computation based on the search terms used. It is also able to perform over 50,000 computations and/or equations. WolframAlpha supports a variety of statistical analyses from ordinary, such as weather prediction, to weights and measurements, to scientific analysis of research-oriented data sets. Results can be presented in a standard search results display or in a variety of displays (visualizations), such as pie charts, graphs, and images, that can be downloaded as PDFs or shared across social media sites.

For a simple example, enter "weather" along with your location and a date. WolframAlpha will display all of the weather data it has for that date in that location in a very easy-to-read format (see Figure 2.2). For more examples to get you started, check out the examples page (http://www .wolframalpha.com/examples/). (We'll investigate WolframAlpha in more detail in Chapter 5.)

▷ Figure 2.2: Weather Data for Seattle for 2008

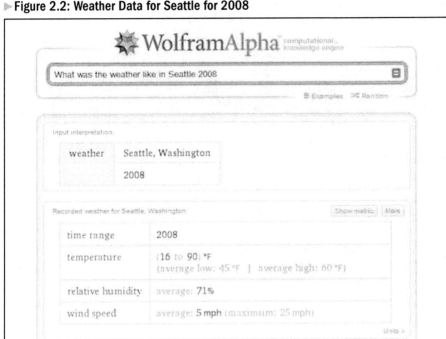

Source: Wolfram | Alpha LLC. 2010. http://www.wolframalpha.com/input/?i=What+was+the+weather+like+in+Seattle+in+2008.

Google News Timeline

The Google News Timeline (http://newstimeline.googlelabs.com/) is still considered a "labs" project and is therefore subject to significant change at any time. Because it's a "labs" project, many librarians we've encountered have no idea that it even exists. Let's take a look at what it does.

Many folks who look to Google to search for news content generally head over to Google News (http://news.google.com/), which presents search results in the standard relevancy-ranked list. However, this doesn't necessarily show how a story has developed over time. This is where Google News Timeline comes in. This service places results in a timeline, with the most recent stories on the right of the screen and older stories on the left. Searchers can then use the left and right arrow buttons at the top of the timeline to scroll into the past or bring up the most current results. (Google doesn't yet have the ability to search into the future, though we're sure they're working on it somewhere!) This way a searcher can see how a story has developed over time and possibly even find both the first and the most recent news items posted online about the topic. (Google News Timeline is another service we'll cover in more detail in Chapter 5.)

► USE MULTIMEDIA SEARCHING

Multimedia searching encompasses searching for all types of media formats, including images, audio, and video. Let's briefly take a look at some of your search options for these types.

Images

A variety of tools exist to search for images across the web by file type, within specific domains, and via sites that search only specific file formats. Both Google Images (http://images.google.com/) and Bing Images (http://www.bing.com/images) search across the general web and offer various filters with which you can limit your results. For example, in Google Images you can limit your results by color (black and white or color only, or a specific color), image type (face, photo, clip art, or line drawing), or size (icon, large, medium, larger than, or specific dimension).

For those looking for images that they can confidently reuse without the threat of a copyright lawsuit, Compfight (http://compfight.com/) is one of our search engines of choice. Although you can search within Flickr and limit those results to only images that include a Creative Commons (CC) license, Compfight offers a much simpler and more user-friendly interface. Just enter your search terms, and then limit your results to images that have a CC license or allow for commercial use. You can also limit your search to just the tags on an image or to any text associated with the image. (We'll discuss Flickr's metadata properties in an exercise in Chapter 5.)

Picsearch (http://www.picsearch.com/) indexes over two billion images and animations from across the web. It has some unique results filters, such as "only images with faces," and the ability to limit your results to just portrait, landscape, or square images. You can also limit your results to just animated images. Finally, most image hosting/editing sites, such as Photobucket (http://photobucket.com/), Shutterfly (http://www.shutterfly.com/), Flickr (http://www.flickr.com/), and Picassa (http://picasa.google.com/), and even Facebook (http://www.facebook.com/), provide the ability to search within their sites for images.

Audio

Searching for audio files and podcasts across the web is challenging, given that there is really only one central storage site: Apple's iTunes. Neither Bing nor Google offers a quick search for these kinds of files nor is it easy to access their metadata. Embedded metadata (information coded within a file format) is not readily available or often used when it does exist; podcast searching relies on word of mouth, social media, and niche search sites, such as PodcastAlley.com.

Video

With more than 48 hours' worth of new content being uploaded to YouTube every minute and more than three billion views daily ("Thanks, YouTube Community, for Two BIG Gifts on Our Sixth Birthday!"; http://youtube-global.blogspot.com/2011/05/thanks-youtube-community-for-two-big.html), it is no surprise that video searching is getting a lot of attention these days. There are a number of video search engines; we'll take a brief look at two: Google Videos and Blinkx.

Google Videos (http://video.google.com/) tends to index user-created content more than any other kind of content. Search results come from sites such as YouTube, Metacafe, blip.tv, break.com, and Dailymotion. However, this isn't to say that you won't see results from sites such as ABC News and the *Wall Street Journal*. Search results can be filtered by length, date, when created, quality, with closed captions, and by source.

Indexing content from different sources, Blinkx (http://www.blinkx.com/) provides results generally from the more "traditional" media sources, such as People.com, Hulu, the Associated Press, and MSNBC. YouTube, the video Goliath that it is, is also represented. Although results limiters are pretty much nonexistent, Blinkx does offer the ability to browse videos by category a lá the Yahoo! of old.

▶ USE SOCIAL SEARCHING

Social searching can be looked at in two ways. The first is simply the searching of social media websites for content that can be limited to a particular domain (e.g., Twitter's search, Facebook's search), across the whole of the social web, or within a selected group (FriendFeed). This type of social searching is already embedded into many searches. Google displays tweets and blog posts along with its standard results. Bing Social works in a similar fashion. Twitter (http://twitter.com/) has both an advanced search and a simple search, providing a wealth of search options from searching by topic to searching for tweets (posts) by specific users across the entirety of all tweets. Of course, Twitter's search is limited to Twitter and does not encompass the span of social media sites.

The other way of looking at social searching is the ability to have what your online "friends" have done (tweet a link, bookmark a website, etc.) impact the way in which results are presented to you. One of Google's more recent views on search is that the more results can be customized to an individual searcher, the better. One of the ways that customization is being done is by looking at the connection between people online. Here are two simple examples based on our personal experiences.

First, Michael starts by using the +1 feature in Google (http://www.google .com/+1/button/). When he finds a result that he believes is particularly noteworthy, he clicks a small +1 icon next to that result. Then, when others who are connected to him online, through services such as Google Buzz, search for similar terms a result that's gotten a +1 from Michael will be ranked higher because that other person, in theory, trusts his judgment.

Another example shows it going the other direction. Michael is connected to his cataloger coworker Emily through a variety of online services such as Twitter. When he searches for "RDA" in Google, one of the first results to appear is the RDA Toolkit. Underneath that result it is reported that Emily has posted a link to that site on her Twitter account. This connection increases the relevancy of the result for Michael because of the connection he and Emily have.

In this way a social search is not just searching the content of the Social Web but also using the connections among individuals in the Social Web to affect the results of a web search.

► USE SEMANTIC SEARCHING

Unlike your standard web search, which generally is just basic keyword matching, semantic search involves constructing searches in which context is known or implied. Many of the search tools like Bing and Google that harvest or use information (data) semantically fall into one or more categories. Both Google and Bing do have features that are more Semantic Web–like than other features, such as the recipe search. Both offer recipes, with Bing at a

Glance (http://www.bing.com/explore), a suite of features within Bing, providing grouped searches, social search (Twitter), and contextual information such as reviewed recipes, ingredients lists, local cooking classes, and photos of the final product.

Bing

Bing also provides a list of related searches that are based on Semantic Web technologies, specifically through utilizing Natural Language Query, which treats words as phrases as they would be spoken; for example, questions are viewed as questions, not as a string of keywords. Bing at a Glance lists dictionaries, events, and recipes and has a link to search the statistical search engine WolframAlpha, all searchable from within Bing. Each of these links has explanatory text to guide the user to choosing the correct subset of content available through Bing. Semantic Web features location-based searching, including traffic and weather, maps containing user-generated content, and, in the basic search results, sublinks, additional links from a website, allowing users to drill deeper for results within a specific site (vertical searching).

Google's Rich Snippets

Google's Rich Snippets is a mechanism for web editors to embed contextual information such as reviews into websites, making for a Semantic Web experience. In Chapter 5, we will focus on Rich Snippets in more detail. In terms of searching, Rich Snippets offers value-added content by providing ratings and reviews as part of the descriptive text accompanying search results. Ratings and reviews can be useful, especially when looking for specific services or products. Data from Rich Snippets is folded into the existing search display; there is currently no way to limit search results to only those webpages with support for Rich Snippets.

▶3

PLANNING

▶ **Develop a Plan**

▶ **Determine Your Resources**

▶ **Find Funding**

▶ **Develop a Sustainability Plan**

▶ **Communicate and Market Your Project**

The Semantic and Social Web projects chosen for this book are practical in nature, stable, yet still on the leading edge of technology. As with all projects for implementation, the scope can be as large or as small as you would like. For some projects the initial work can be done in an afternoon or two, but continuing to create data (such as enriching Flickr data for your images) should be an ongoing process. Other projects, such as implementing RDA in a library's catalog, will require much more initial training and a plan for implementation.

Planning technology projects is no different from planning any other project; they still need to be planned in order to be successful. Libraries are traditionally very good at planning projects; however, technology projects can sometimes be challenging. Planning doesn't involve overthinking, nor does it require planning every tiny detail. A good plan can evolve and adapt to meet challenges that arise along the way.

However, taking a little bit of time to plan and set a project in motion will ensure the project goes more smoothly and more efficiently. Project plans can be very complex or relatively simple, depending on its overall scope. There are a lot of good project tools out there; Google Docs (http://docs .google.com/) and Google Groups (http://groups.google.com/) can be used collaboratively to manage a project. Social media sites like Facebook can be used similarly, in addition to sites and software specifically designed for project management, like Basecamp (http://basecamphq.com/).

Project management focuses on identifying the three important and interdependent criteria for success: time, resources, and cost. For example, if your project has a short time frame, you will need more resources (possibly staff time or faster computers); you may need to hire or outsource some of the work. If your project has little funding, you may be relying on committees or volunteers to do the work; in that case, your time frame may be longer, because staff do not have as much time to commit. If you have a lot of resources, such as pages or volunteers, you may be able to accomplish more within a shorter time frame. (As the old joke goes: Good, fast, or cheap, pick any two.)

One of the goals of project management is to determine the roles that time, resources, and cost play on your project. Project management involves the following components:

- ▸ Identify a project.
- ▸ Determine the scope of the project. Technology projects are often victims of scope creep, that is, the project escalates beyond the original intent.
- ▸ Determine a time frame. Projects without time frames or target deadlines just become lower priorities in the course of life. They will drag on infinitely.
- ▸ Develop a process.
- ▸ Determine resources needed—what you have already and what you will need. Resources include people, capital, and equipment.
- ▸ Determine an outcome. What is the goal of your project? What is your end result? How will you measure success?
- ▸ Write a project plan.

▸ DEVELOP A PLAN

To finish a project and get it launched before the technology is obsolete, you will need to determine what is achievable in the desired time frame. Upgrades, enhancements, tweaking from usability studies, and feedback may all become part of phase two or the next project. As ideas come up, you will need to determine what is feasible and what is outside of the project but may be a worthy second or follow-up project. Getting that all in writing and getting key players and management to sign off on it are essential parts of good project management.

A written plan is an essential part of good project planning and will include:

1. Concept
2. Scale and scope
3. Reason for project

4. Stakeholders (who authorizes, who administers)
5. Resources (staff, time, cost factors)
6. Process (how will it get done, who will do it, from implementation through launch)
7. Milestones and goals
8. Evaluation and testing
9. Deadline, target time frame, and launch

▶ DETERMINE YOUR RESOURCES

Resources for a technology project include both what you already have as well as what you need. Look carefully at the requirements of the project to determine what resources you have already and what you need to add. Of course, it's quite possible that you will have to "make do" with the resources at hand.

In that case, carefully evaluate the resources you have and whether they are sufficient to complete the project. If your computers do not meet the minimum system requirements of a particular project, the project may be impossible. If you do not have IT staff to help you, do you have staff within your library who can learn to install and run the software or can learn to utilize the site in such a way as needed by your project?

For example, if you are looking to offer some computational abilities to your users by adding a customized WolframAlpha widget to your website, do you have someone who can learn what is needed to create the widget and embed it on your site? Do they have time to do it? If not, will your project be a high enough priority to fit within the time frame? Determining what you will need for the project is crucial—especially if there is no funding.

▶ FIND FUNDING

Given the state of many library budgets these days, funding for new technology projects may be limited. Check out grants offered through the Institute of Museum and Library Services and any consortia or statewide organizations you're connected to. ALA and other library-specific organizations may also offer support through either grants or awards or training or resources.

Stay involved with your organizations, and network with people within those organizations who are interested in the types of technology projects you are planning. It may be possible to pool resources, tapping into collective knowledge and skills. Funding impacts other decisions, too. It may be that you can upgrade computers or parts rather than purchase new items; you may be able to find surplus or used items that meet the needs of the project.

You may find it cheaper to rent equipment or resources, too; it truly depends on what kind of funding you have.

Sometimes what appears to be the cheapest isn't, and staff time is often over-looked in considering the cost for a project. Even something as theoretically inconsequential as the cost of electricity to run servers is often overlooked in terms of technology projects. You do not have to make a list of needs right down to the wattage required for a project; the questions in the following sidebar will help you stay focused. If you are trying to justify the cost of out-sourcing, cost analysis is important.

To Justify a Cost, Consider These Questions

1. How does the item fit with the mission of the library? Is it important to your library and how?
2. What functionalities do we need for our project? What is on our "shopping list"?
3. What resources and funds do we have available? Do they meet the basic system requirements?
4. What is the product's reputation? For software, you should always consider the product's maturity; there are many new products that come out every day, and whether or not they will still be around in a few years is important.
5. What about testing, support, and maintenance?
6. Is it scalable? Will it grow with us?
7. Is it secure? Are there any security issues?
8. How will you measure success?

▶ DEVELOP A SUSTAINABILITY PLAN

Few technology projects have a finite deliverable product, and, as technologies change and the role of libraries in society evolves, software evolves. Upgrades will become available. Security issues will develop and need to be patched. Regardless of the reason, upgrades need to be factored in as part of the continuing maintenance of the product.

This ongoing maintenance is a very important reason to develop a plan for sustainability. Over the course of this project's life (and you may have no idea how long that will be) what needs to happen to keep the product useful, relevant, and up-to-date? Who will maintain it? If it involves creating content, who will create content? What training is needed to teach the staff and users how to use the software and how to maintain it and keep it current? Factoring in a plan for sustainability will encourage the success of the project.

▶ COMMUNICATE AND MARKET YOUR PROJECT

As your project is building out, you will need to communicate frequently with your project team about progress, goals, timelines, benchmarks, and target dates. Not all communication needs to be face to face; much of it can be handled through e-mail, IM, conference calls, discussion forums, project spaces like wikis or Google Docs, and other online formats. However, some face-to-face communication is always desirable, especially at high points in the project. Having a kickoff party or meeting is a great idea in that it is a way to introduce team members to each other and for you to set the tone of the team. It is also a way to generate some enthusiasm, answer any questions that may arise, and help cement the team as a unit.

Face-to-face meetings are also important to celebrate successes. This is an often overlooked part of project management. Most people want to know that they are doing a good job; success is a powerful motivator. Conversely, if your project is struggling, a face-to-face meeting may be just what you need to solve problems, rededicate the team, and get the project back on track. Finally, the launch is not only a time to promote your new project but also a celebration. You want to celebrate the success of your work (and your team) and acknowledge the work that went into the project.

Throughout the course of your project you want to communicate not only with those directly involved in the project implementation but also with the staff who may be involved later in the project—either in the launch or the maintenance aspect of the project. Additionally, there may be promotional opportunities throughout the project life cycle that are perfect opportunities to share "what's coming up" at the library. Social media can be an excellent tool to keep patrons and staff informed about the project's progress. Usability testing can also be a way to drive interest in your new project in that you can appeal to those who are interested in trying new technologies—the early adopters.

Marketing happens at all stages of your project. You may be handed a project that you need to sell to your team; you may find a project that you want to do and need to sell it to your library's administration. You may not even have a team and need to sell your project to a group of potential volunteers—who will hopefully offer to help you after learning about your wonderful new project! Marketing is about not only successfully promoting your project to your staff, your patrons, and the public but also getting your team, your administration, and outside parties such as the library's friends group on board.

▶4

SOCIAL MECHANICS

- ▶ **Work with Your Systems/IT Department**
- ▶ **Use Committees and Meetings**
- ▶ **Identify Appropriate Staff**
- ▶ **Create Buy-In and Good Public Relations**

Staff resources are one of the most overlooked factors in a library technology plan. Staff are often stretched thin and may not have the time to learn a new system or a new programming language; they may not have the skills needed to install and configure a complex software system. It is important to carefully evaluate your staff resources, especially if you have limited tech support. If you do not have tech support within your library, you may need to look for help across your campus, your consortium, school system, or state. Before you begin a project, you have to know who will do the work. It may be that you have staff within your library who have the skills or aptitude to learn; in that case, you may just need to factor in time to get them (and perhaps, even yourself) up to speed!

▶WORK WITH YOUR SYSTEMS/IT DEPARTMENT

If you are fortunate to have a systems/IT department to assist you, either within your library or on your campus, they will be an essential resource. If you cultivate a good relationship with your systems/IT staff, projects will go more smoothly. It is important to consult with them before you write your definitive technology plan, but, at the same time, you need to have a clear idea of what you want to accomplish and what resources you have available. They may provide you with project planning resources; they may know of other projects on campus or in the library that you can "piggyback" on; and they may also be able to point you to resources or even potential red flags. Do some preliminary research so that you can have an educated conversation with your systems/IT department when the time comes.

As much as possible, you want to be able to speak a common language with your IT/systems staff; you need to understand the basics of what you are asking of them. If you have a deadline, they need to know that up front. They also will need to know the priority of the project; the priority may be set by administration, by the time of the year (perhaps you want to roll out new services or web features during the summer), by other projects that are higher (or lower) priority, or other factors that you and the IT/systems department determine. The initial meeting with the IT/systems staff will help inform your choice and project management plan; depending on whether they do work for you or just serve as tech support, they will be an important resource throughout the project process.

► USE COMMITTEES AND MEETINGS

Libraries often function through the work of committees; sometimes these committees are just project working groups. In terms of project working groups, it is critical to the success of the project that everyone involved gets information and stays up-to-date. Everyone should know their part of the project and the milestones. Committee meetings can celebrate milestones and targets in addition to discussing the business at hand. While it may seem obvious, your project team needs to see the rewards of their efforts and celebrate their successes. However, you should never meet just to meet! Each meeting should have an agenda with action items; this is especially crucial in a technology project.

Not all meetings have to be face to face; this is determined by the needs of the committee members. Depending on the scale of the project, some project groups may have subgroups (PR/marketing, implementation, testing, etc.). The bigger the project, the more important communication is; each project should have a project manager. The project manager's job is to keep the project on track and, when snags occur, to evaluate what needs to be done.

► IDENTIFY APPROPRIATE STAFF

Finding the appropriate staff is an important part of project management. Most projects work best when clear-cut duties are assigned to specific staff. This provides accountability and helps ensure that all of the critical duties of the project are done. It also helps alleviate overlap and confusion over "who is doing what." Assigning duties and responsibilities works not only with individuals but also within committees. Assigning specific tasks, duties, and responsibilities does not prevent collaboration; instead, it can make collaboration more successful. Work can be brought before the group by the individual, and from there collaborative thought and work can happen, with the individual then responsible for implementing changes based on group consensus.

Key individuals in a technology project team include:

- ▶ Project leader or manager to oversee the project plan and team development, communication, team progress and plan evaluation, team motivation, conflict resolution and decision making, scheduling, securing appropriate approvals (stakeholders, sponsors), and working with vendors, among other tasks
- ▶ Sponsors, who can be advocates, funding partners, administration, library boards, and/or a friends of the library group
- ▶ Team members (depending on scope of project, some members may cover multiple roles):
  - ▸ Tech support for installation, configuration, coding, server requirements, systems or IT work, testing, and security issues
  - ▸ Designer for graphics and web functionality (can also help with PR, marketing, and usability testing)
  - ▸ Marketing, PR, and communications
  - ▸ Web services, including implementation and usability testing
  - ▸ Training and documentation writing
- ▶ Stakeholders, including everyone listed plus any outside liaisons (such as faculty on campus who are interested in the project and marketing teams within your consortia)

▶ CREATE BUY-IN AND GOOD PUBLIC RELATIONS

One factor that can make or break even the best technology project is lack of buy-in. If you do not have the support from your administration or systems/IT staff, the chances of your project succeeding are very limited. Working around resistance is hard and may actually kill your project, so get buy-in from the start. While it is great to have wildly enthusiastic supporters, not everyone has to be a cheerleader.

It is also possible that someone who is initially resistant will become an advocate for your project. Projects often involve something new—*change.* Some people find change to be challenging, while others embrace it. Nowhere does this seem to be truer than with technology. You will encounter early adopters, some who are interested but cautious, and others who are unwilling to embrace the new technology unless it is forced upon them.

You will need to be not only an advocate for your project but also a little bit of a cheerleader. If you have communications, marketing, or PR staff (or staff with these aptitudes), reach out to them for help. Reach out to the early adopters and to those interested in technology; is there some role they can play in your project? Perhaps they can help with testing, which will not only help your project team but also provide an opportunity for staff to learn about the new product and, possibly, start evangelizing for you.

Don't limit yourself to specific staff; consider all staff and users. "Sneak peeks" and special previews can entice the curious to take a look at what you are doing. While you may want to limit the size of the project working group to keep it focused, letting all staff and users know what is going on and giving them a role in the process will make them a part of it and will help ensure the success of the project in the long term. Make the project not "your" project, but "our" project; this is key to getting buy-in.

Market throughout the duration of the project; don't leave it to the end with the launch. Send out teasers via newsletters, blogs, and social media sites; "sneak previews" can help drum up interest. You may need to develop a marketing plan as part of the project management plan, especially if you want to do a large-scale marketing campaign. There are so many ways to market new technology projects, from banners or badges on websites to kickoff launch parties. Truly, you are limited only by your resources and budget!

5

IMPLEMENTATION

- ▶ Track and Start Trends Using Social Media
- ▶ Use Social Search to Track Reputation
- ▶ Find Hidden Content Online
- ▶ Search for Reusable Online Content
- ▶ Explore Data and Statistics through WolframAlpha
- ▶ Create Searchable Metadata in Flickr
- ▶ Semanticize Simple Data with Google's Rich Snippets
- ▶ Contribute Linked Data to a Civil War Project

Now that we've given you a solid grasp of the technologies involved in both social and semantic search, in this chapter we will explore a variety of search and Semantic Web–oriented projects. Most of these will require little technical knowledge, while some will require a bit more. Through these projects, you will find new and innovative ideas and tips that will reenergize your searching, hone your technical abilities, enhance your understanding of the Semantic and Social Webs, prepare your content for the Semantic Web, and even provide some ideas you can incorporate into your library's web presence and social media efforts. You will become a better searcher by developing a more cohesive and effective web presence, ensuring that you are able to not only find the most relevant results for your patrons but also have a role in creating results and providing access to them.

Note on Illustrations

Many of the screenshots that are integral to illustrating the implementation processes described in this chapter are too detailed for the print medium and appear instead on the book's companion website. As you read this chapter, go to http://www.alatechsource.org/techset/semanticweb/ to access these additional illustrations where noted within the text.

▶ TRACK AND START TRENDS USING SOCIAL MEDIA

Why Trends Are Important

Trends are popular topics, events, people, and places that are being discussed on the Internet, typically through social media, rising to the top of search results. Trends can be viral (shared and spread from one person to another), and often they provide just a glimpse into the collective knowledge, breaking news, and cultural interest of the people on the web.

Social media is often ahead of traditional media, frequently breaking news stories (Zack Whittaker, "Why Twitter Inherently Reports News before Traditional Media," *ZDnet*, July 26, 2011, http://www.zdnet.com/blog/igeneration/why-twitter-inherently-reports-news-before-traditional-media/11668). During natural disasters such as the Japanese earthquake of 2011, people were posting videos, photos, blog posts, and tweets; some were from those directly affected by the earthquake, and others were in response to the earthquake. Many relief agencies and volunteer efforts used social media to get the word out about how to help and contribute; news agencies also used social media to get news out quickly. Google created a people locator whereby families could list who was missing and who had been found; the people locator was then tweeted, blogged, and shared on Facebook by numerous organizations, companies, and individuals. In the days following the Japanese earthquake, trending topics in Twitter included Japan, tsunami, and #prayforjapan, among others; eight of the top ten trending topics on March 11, 2011, were related to Japan (Lauren Dugan, "Twitter in Shock after Japanese Earthquake," *AllTwitter* [blog], March 11, 2011, http://www.mediabistro.com/alltwitter/twitter-in-shock-after-japanese-earthquake_b4382).

Politics are often trending topics; people use social media both to keep abreast of the latest information and to communicate with others within political movements. Social media has played active roles in Iranian elections and the Egyptian revolution. Trends are also reflected in content posted on social media sites, such as Facebook, Flickr, Twitter, and YouTube; trends are not limited to one specific type of social media, although Twitter is one of the more popular sites for trends.

Twitter trends are indicated by hashtags, for example, #prayforjapan. Hashtags in Twitter are a way to provide some contextual information to a tweet; users add a hashtag to a keyword, such as a subject, name, or location. Hashtags are searchable and can even be subscribed to. Users attending conferences and other events will often add a specific hashtag to their posts so that they can easily colocate posts about that topic. Other examples of hashtags include #library (a subject), #FF (for Follow Friday, a Friday occurrence in which Twitter users acknowledge and recognize their peers on Twitter), #alamw2010 (ALA Midwinter 2010 conference), and #smmanners (social media manners, a discussion group).

Being able to track trends can be a valuable tool for librarians. Trends can be used to help patrons find breaking news, learn about pop culture, and find discussions about topics such as politics or new technology products. Librarians use social media to talk about e-books (such as changes in licensing for e-books, new readers, and platforms), post new books and resources, share information about free webinars and training, and much more.

How to Find Trends

Finding trends is easy. Twitter and Twitter tools such as Brizzly (http://brizzly .com/) have sidebar sections dedicated to tracking trends. Additionally, Brizzly allows its users to add contextual information to explain why a topic is trending. This contextual information is then displayed to all Brizzly users; under each trending topic there is a "Why?" link to the contextual information.

Examples of trends that you may have seen include:

▶ Color-based Facebook avatars (pink for Breast Cancer Awareness or green for Iranian revolutionaries)
▶ Blog posts on a specific subject often answering a series of questions (100 Things about Me)
▶ Twitter hashtags such as #musicmondays (what music you are listening to), #fridayreads (what book you are reading), and #frifoto (photos posted on Friday on Twitter)

Finding Trends on Twitter

In 2010, Twitter began to summarize trends through its Year in Review (http://yearin review.twitter.com/), dividing trends into categories such as new celebrities, top trends (including top ten news, people, events, movies, as well as hashtags) for the year, most powerful, and most retweeted. The Year in Review is a good snapshot of a year's top trends.

How to Track Trends in Twitter

Every search in Twitter creates an RSS feed. Hashtags can be saved as searches and then subscribed to via an RSS reader like Google Reader or embedded into existing websites in order to provide real-time comments and feedback about particular topics. The RSS feed for a hashtag is http://twitter.com/ #!/search?q=%23_topic, where "topic" is the keyword you are searching for.

For example, for the keyword "libraries," the feed is http://twitter.com/#!/ search?q=%23_libraries.

Searching for hashtags in Twitter can uncover a treasure trove of hidden content. The keyword assigned might make little sense outside of the group using it, but knowing what the hashtag is can open a wealth of content. Specialized sites such as Hashtag Wiki (http://www.hashtag.org/) track hashtags, their uses, who uses them, and the time frame. Twitter's own advanced search tool (http://search.twitter.com/advanced) provides a search box for hashtags (as well as keywords and username) in addition to a variety of other searches.

There are also various third-party services online that can help you track memes (virally spread topics; *Wikipedia*, "Meme," http://en.wikipedia.org/ w/index.php?title=Meme&oldid=435030502; accessed November 29, 2011) via Twitter. One is TweetMeme (http://tweetmeme.com/), which shows numbers of retweets—the number of times a tweet has been reposted by other Twitter users (an indicator of popularity)—when the tweet became popular, number of comments it got, and who posted it originally (i.e., the source). If you are logged in and have linked TweetMeme to your Twitter account, clicking on the retweet button of a particular post will push it out to your users. Additionally, tweets are organized by community/topic, such as technology, as well as by media (photos, video, news). Although there is no search box, the homepage sorts posts chronologically.

Another tool is Twitt(url)y (http://twitturly.com/), which has a search interface in addition to showing what is popular, number of retweets, and a choice of seeing photos, video, news, or everything. Other tools that provide chronological lists of trends and searching include Trendistic (http:// trendistic.indextank.com/), Trendsmap (http://trendsmap.com/), and What the Trend (http://www.whatthetrend.com/). Trendistic displays trends in a timeline, showing the percentage of tweets for a particular topic. Trendsmap displays trends via a map (local, regional, worldwide) and also ranks trends breaking globally; videos are displayed in separate lists. What the Trend provides contextual information about why trends are popular, in addition to displaying trends in chronological order or by location or via search.

Beyond Twitter

A number of other news sources, blogs, discussion forums, and image and video websites also highlight the most popular or what is trending:

▹ Google Trends (http://www.google.com/trends) searches trends across the web, including blogs and news sites.

▶ YouTube Trends (http://www.youtube.com/trendsdashboard) sorts by most shared and most viewed videos at YouTube.

▶ Delicious (http://www.delicious.com/popular/) searches for popular bookmarks.

▶ Facebook's 2010 Memology (http://www.facebook.com/blog.php?post =466369142130) looks back at the most popular status updates on Facebook in 2010.

▶ StumbleUpon, a website referral and rating service for websites (http://www.stumbleupon.com/discover/most-popular/10/), lists its most popular websites.

Trend Apps for Mobile

If you use any of the Twitter tools for mobile, you can always find trends using Twitter's interface; however, some tools specifically search for trends. Both the Android Market and iTunes stores offer a variety of trends apps—from local businesses to news to fashion and just about everything in between:

▶ Hot Trend Search (http://www.androidapps.com/apps/396751-hot-trend-search-lost-link-search) searches Google Trends for the Android.

▶ Hitpad (http://www.hitpad.com/) searches and displays latest topics, including video, tweets, and news for the iPad.

▶ Twitscoop (http://twitscoop.com/) is a robust Twitter tool to find and follow trends ("what's buzzing on Twitter in real time") for the iPhone, iPod touch, and iPad.

Ideas to Get You Started

Why would you want to start a trend? It is a great tool to promote an event; it is also a good way to get feedback and comments from users, too! One of the easiest ways to start a trend is to create a hashtag to be used in Twitter for a public event. This hashtag needs to be shared in all formats: word of mouth, on print material, and in social media—not just Twitter, but others as well. Everything that you create for or as part of an event should include the hashtag on it somewhere. You want people not only to find your event by the tag but also to reshare using the tag, thus starting a potentially viral explosion!

What other trends might a library consider starting? Here are a few examples to get you thinking:

▶ Write a story on Twitter using a specific hashtag to publicize a reading theme, young adult program, or literacy program.

▶ Have a scavenger hunt in the library using photographs posted to Flickr using a specific tag, and post clues on Twitter using a hashtag.

- ▶ Put together a digital scrapbook on Flickr or Facebook using a specific tag.
- ▶ Create a hashtag in Twitter that patrons can use to indicate books they're currently reading.
- ▶ Watch for breaking local or library-related news and communicate information to patrons.
- ▶ Use trending topics to identify resources for reader's advisories or to find new content.
- ▶ Use a hashtag to create an online discussion group at Twitter.
- ▶ Use a hashtag to pull together content for a class or workshop (e.g., in Delicious, bookmark resources and create a tag just for that bundle of links, such as business_101_workshop).

Ideas for how to use trends on the Internet are endless. Certainly they are a great way to find new content and resources to share, but they are also an incredible tool for staying informed of current affairs, creating and participating in discussions, gathering feedback from users, and much more. Using trends is an underutilized search method, yet we are expected to remain aware of what's new, what's popular, and what's emerging. Why not tap into the global network to achieve that?

▶USE SOCIAL SEARCH TO TRACK REPUTATION

Once your library is online via social media services, someone is going to start asking, "just how much reach are we achieving as a result of our efforts?" Knowing how many followers your library account has is a good place to start, but it doesn't really answer some of the more important questions. For example, your library may have 1,000 Twitter followers, but are they engaging you in conversation or passing along any of the information you're providing? Are your patrons mentioning you in their blogs or rating you in Foursquare? Having a lot of followers or "friends" is not the only way to judge your online effectiveness. Let's take a look at some of the other ways you can begin to answer questions such as these.

Google Searches

One of the simplest ways of finding out whether others are mentioning your library online is to perform a simple Google search. For example, Michael is at the Nebraska Library Commission, so he's interested in people mentioning Nebraska libraries. Periodically he heads over to Google and searches for "nebraska library" just to see if there are any mentions. Someone at the Omaha Public Library would do a more specific search on "omaha public library," for example. To be sure you're seeing the latest results, limit your results to those from the past month, week, or 24 hours, depending on how often you do this kind of search.

Beyond just doing a simple keyword search, look for results that are a little more specific:

- ▶ Search Google News for mentions of your library in the media.
- ▶ Search for links back to your library's website using "link:Library's URL" to see who's linking their website to yours. (Type in the library's URL in place of "Library'sURL"—no need to include "http://" or "www."—and add "–link:Library'sURL" to the search so you don't receive results from your own site.)
- ▶ Search Google Blog to see what's being said in social media.
- ▶ Perform other searches based on variations of your library's name. For example, if you're the Topeka and Shawnee County Public Library, you might search for "topeka library" and "tscpl" along with the full library name. You can also search for the names of library branches.

All of the results from searches such as these will be useful. However, you may already be thinking that performing these searches on a regular basis will become time-consuming very quickly. This is where Google Alerts (http://www.google.com/alerts) comes in.

Google Alerts

Google Alerts is a free service (requiring just a free Google account in order to be able to manage the alerts long term) that allows you to set up your search and then have the results sent to you automatically on a schedule of your choosing via one of several methods. For example, your library can set up all of the previously listed example searches, and then, instead of having to reenter them weekly, have Google automatically reperform the search once a week and send you an e-mail containing only previously unseen results. If you have searches that you need to do on a regular basis, this is a tool that you ought to be using. Let's take a look at a couple of sample Google Alerts.

Once again, let's say we're the Topeka and Shawnee County Public Library, and we're interested in what people are saying about our library on the web in general. The first thing we need to do is determine our search terms. Although Google Alerts gives us only a single search box in which to work, all of Google's search syntax works. So, keeping in mind that not everyone may mention the library using its full name, we'll set up a slightly complex search:

"topeka and shawnee county public library" or "tscpl" or (topeka and library)

This will find any mention of the library's full name, the commonly used abbreviation, and mentions of the town and library in the same content. (You could also create a single alert for each of these searches, but why not take advantage of your online search syntax skills?)

Next, we need to decide the type of search (Everything, News, Blogs, Video, or Discussion), how often we want to be notified of new results (As it happens, Once a day, or Once a week), volume (Only the best results or All results), and whether we'd like the results e-mailed to us or delivered as an RSS feed. For this example, we'll choose Everything, Once a week, All results, and via e-mail.

As you type in your search words and set your options, a sample set of results is displayed and updated on the right side of the screen. Figure 5.1 shows our settings and sample results as they stand right now.

Now all we need to do is click "CREATE ALERT" to have Google start doing the work. Based on this example, in a week we'll start receiving e-mails that contain links to the newest search results that match our criteria. Be aware that your first e-mail will probably be longer than the subsequent ones, because the first time out all results will be new.

If you're more of an RSS person than an e-mail person, instead of receiving a weekly e-mail you can choose to receive your results as an RSS feed "as it happens." This is useful if you find your library involved in a significant local

▶ **Figure 5.1: Setting Up a Google Alert**

news story (search News instead of Everything) such as city budget negotiations or a significant book challenge.

You can create a practically unlimited number of Google Alerts, but keep in mind that you're going to have to deal with receiving the results of the alerts you've created. If you create alerts while signed into your Google account, you can return in the future and click the "manage your alerts" link to edit and delete your existing alerts.

While Google Alerts are useful, they're going to get you results only from Google. For many searches Google results are more than enough, but there are other ways to search Social Web content. Let's take a look at some of the other resources out there.

Spezify

The easiest way we can describe Spezify (http://www.spezify.com/) is as a cross between a typical search engine in that it searches across the web and an image-only search engine in that it presents the results in a visual grid-like way. If this isn't clear enough, let's do a quick search to see what we mean before we go any further. Let's search for "topeka library."

To see the results, go to http://www.alatechsource.org/techset/semanticweb/ to access this figure: Spezify Results for "topeka library"

What you see is not just a standard list of results as you would receive from Google or Bing. Instead, Spezify actually pulls content from each of the found websites and presents that content in its own container on the results page. This page can be scrolled up and down and zoomed in and out for a more or less detailed picture of the results. Each of the containers includes a small icon in the upper-left corner indicating the source of the content: Twitter, Facebook, Amazon, Flickr, and eBay, to name just a few.

Try hovering over a particular item. When you do this you'll receive the title of that item. Clicking on an item will refocus the page on that result and provide additional information, including the author's name (if available), the ability to add the results to your favorites (star), the ability to display the Spezify URL for this particular result (link), and a button showing the domain name of the site this result comes from (which, when clicked, will send you to the webpage containing the content). Clicking on the container again will defocus the item and return you to the results list.

Next let's take a look at the silver bar across the top of the page. Here you'll see your search terms along with a set of related terms that Spezify thinks might be relevant to your current search. However, it's important to note that, unlike other search engines with a similar "suggested terms" feature, clicking one of these terms does not add the term to your current search. Instead, it performs a new search on the clicked word. For example, if you were to click the related term "public" you would not get a search for "topeka library public" but a search for just "public."

To the right of the silver bar is a set of five icons: photo, text, video, sound, and tweets. By default all of these are turned on. This means that Spezify is presenting results of all five types. By clicking on an icon you will be turning off that type of results. If you want to know what's being said about your library only on Twitter and Facebook, turn off all the results except for Tweets. (Yes, technically Facebook posts aren't tweets, but as far as Spezify is concerned they're close enough.) As you start turning on and off results types you'll also see your results dynamically change; as results types are removed, the remaining space is quickly filled in by the results type(s) that are still being requested.

> To see our search limited to just tweets, go to http://www.alatechsource.org/techset/semantic web/ to access this figure: Spezify Results for "topeka library" Limited to Tweets

The last three icons in the upper-right bar give you access to any items you've marked as favorites (star), information about Spezify (i), and preferences (wrench). Under preferences you'll find settings for turning on and off search sources, scrolling controls, safe search, the ability to minimize the silver bar, and turn off tool tips.

Visualizing Your Twitter Relationships

Now that we've found a lot of posts from individuals who mention our library, let's look at this from another angle. Are any of these people following the library on social media? Is the library following them? Are they talking to each other, or are any of them talking about a topic that the library might be able to help with? This is the next level of analysis when it comes to tracking the library's online reputation.

Many online services will report to you the number of followers you have and the number of people you follow and track these numbers over time. TwitterCounter (http://www.twittercounter.com/) is just one example. Although a bar chart is a visualization of data, I'm sure we can all agree that it's a pretty boring visualization and hardly taxes today's technology. So, instead of looking at a service like TwitterCounter that just provides numbers and graphs, let's take a look at a different type of visualization, one that displays not only the connections between your library Twitter account and your followers but also the connections that may exist among your followers. Mentionmapp (http://mentionmapp.com/beta/classic/#) does just this.

The interface to this tool is simple, yet the information it provides can be significant. To get started, type in your library's Twitter handle and press enter. For this example we'll use @msulibraries, the account for The Michigan State University Libraries in East Lansing.

To see the results, go to http://www.alatechsource.org/techset/semanticweb/ to access this figure: The mentionmapp of @msulibraries

What Mentionmapp does is scan your account's recent tweets and hashtags, along with those of your followers, and draw a map of the connections. Each line between two entities means that there is a connection. In our example, @msulibraries has recently used the hashtags #msuchi, #lovelansing, and #ff. Hovering over each of the lines connecting two items shows the number of recent mentions of that hashtag. Hovering over the line connecting @msulibraries and another user will show the number of recent interactions between those two users. The lines drawing the connections also have a significance built into them: the thicker the line, the stronger the connection between two entities. You can also click on individual entities to expand their network outward.

Once you get the hang of navigating these connections and interpreting the results, you can begin to draw conclusions from them. Here's one of the most significant connections that you should look for. Let's say that you notice a number of connections between a hashtag being used by several of your followers. From this you could infer that people who follow the library are interested in similar things. The question is, are you, as the library, aware of what that hashtag is all about? Is there an event in town that they're talking about? Is it a new meme being picked up by the students on campus? Whatever it is, is it something that the library can participate in? Remember, Twitter is all about conversation. Don't be afraid to join the conversation, participate in the meme, or offer the library's resources in assistance. By visualizing the connections among the library's followers, it's possible to find new ways to participate in your community.

▶ FIND HIDDEN CONTENT ONLINE

Most of you have used both Google and Bing for basic web searching. In fact, we're confident in saying that pretty much anyone reading this has used one or both of these popular search engines at least once in the past few days. However, we're also confident in saying that many of you have probably not moved much beyond the basic or advanced search pages of either of these services.

In previous chapters we've talked about both of these search engines and some of the more nontraditional services that they offer. Now let's take a look at a scenario that you're likely to come across in a library of any type and see how some of these other services of Google and Bing can be applied.

Google

On Friday, March 11, 2011, the eastern coast of Japan was hit with a massive earthquake, which was followed by a devastating tsunami. The devastation caused by these events was rated in the billions of dollars, resulted in thousands of deaths, created more than 300,000 refugees, and even shifted the earth's axis an estimated 10 cm. As much as the *Wikipedia* website can tell us about these events and the aftermath, and as much as a simple search of Google and Bing can present us with facts and figures, there is more out there to be found.

For example, what were people saying about the events as they happened, and what are they saying today? How were the events portrayed in the news, and how did the portrayal change over time? What firsthand accounts are available online in both audio and video formats? Let's use some of Google's alternative search services to answer these questions.

Google offers several specialized searches that many users are not familiar with. In keeping with our example of the 2011 Japanese quake and tsunami, let's find out what people were saying about the event via Google Blogs, what academics wrote about via Google Scholar, and see how the event was portrayed in the news over time using Google News Timeline.

Google Blogs

There are times when you're interested in what "people" are saying about an event—not necessarily the "official" version of the story or what's being reported in what's known as the "mainstream media," but what the typical man-on-the-street has to say. Sometimes stories break and are discussed on blogs long before the mainstream media gets a hold of the story. In these cases, a search that is specifically focused on blog content can be a much better resource than a general web search engine. This is where Google Blogs (http://blogsearch.google.com/) comes in.

In Google Blogs, let's try a simple search. Type in "2011 japan tsunami" and see what sort of results you get (see Figure 5.2).

First we are presented with blogs specifically related to the topic we're searching for: *Earthquake Japan 2011*, *Japan Tsunami 2011*, and *Japan Tsunami*

▶ **Figure 5.2: Google Blogs Search Results for "2011 japan tsunami"**

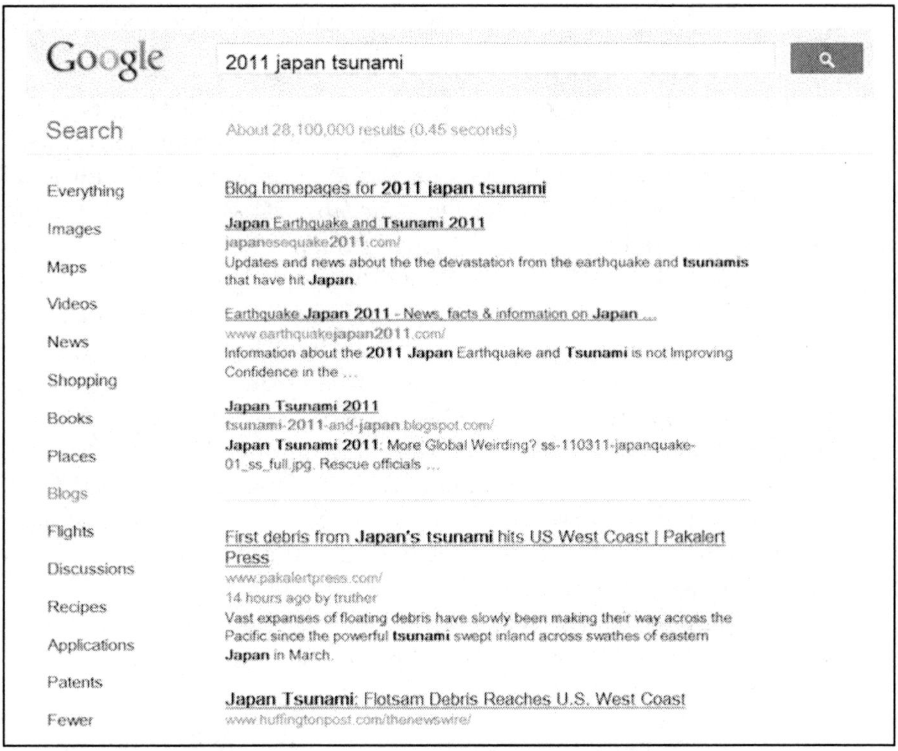

2011 HQ. Below these we're given a list of individual blog posts related to our search. So, depending on the level of detail you're looking for, you can explore blogs whose purpose is to specifically talk about the topic at hand, or you can read posts from bloggers who may generally write about other topics but had something to say about the event.

If you wish to see just blogs about the topic, or just individual posts about the topic, you can click on either the "Posts" or "Homepages" limiters on the left. You can also limit to just homepages by clicking on the "Related blogs about…" link at the top of the results list.

Other limiting options listed on the left allow you to narrow your results to a time period ranging from "Any time" (the default) to the "Past 10 minutes" for extremely up-to-date results. You can also limit the results to a specific date range, and you can sort your results by relevance (the default) or by date.

To see the rest of the options available in Google Blogs, head on over to the Blogs Advanced Search at http://blogsearch.google.com/blogsearch/advanced_blog_search. (Clicking the "Advanced search" link at the top-right of the results screen will send you to the general Google advanced search, *not* the advanced blogs search.) Here there are more limiters that you can add to your search:

> **with these words in the blog title:** Keywords entered into this field must appear as part of the title of the blog listed in the results. This is used to search mainly for whole blogs about a topic as opposed to individual posts. However, if you're looking for librarians talking about the tsunami, you could specify "2011 japan tsunami" as your general search keywords and have "librarian" in the title of the blog.

> **at this URL:** If you know the URL of a particular blog you would like to search or would like to limit your results to a particular top-level domain such as .edu, enter that here. For example, adding ".edu" would limit your results to only blogs hosted at colleges and universities.

> **blogs and posts written by:** Most blogs have authors listed for the blog as a whole and for individual posts. Unfortunately, sometimes the full name isn't listed or a pseudonym is used. However, don't underestimate the possibilities of this field, especially if you're interested in what a popular blogger has said about a topic.

> **post written/posts written between:** This is the same as the date range limiters on the search results page but presented in a slightly different format.

There isn't much more you need to know to make the most of Google's blog search engine. If you're interested in exploring it more, why not give it a try by searching for the name of your library and see what people are saying.

Google Scholar

Possibly going from one extreme to another, let's now switch from considering what the general public had to say to what scholars have to say. Many times, or more often than not for most academic librarians, you may be looking for scholarly research that has been done on a topic. Although it may seem too soon for such content to exist for an event that happened just six months prior to the writing of this book, there is already a surprising amount of content available. With this in mind, let's take a look at Google Scholar (http://scholar.google.com/).

To get started, let's repeat our basic search: "2011 japan tsunami." What you'll quickly notice is that the first few results aren't exactly recent; some are from 1997 and even 1975 on our initial search. The problem here is that the keyword "2011" doesn't necessarily imply a date. As far as we could tell, in the 1975 article, 2011 was the copyright date listed on the page the result linked us to. So, to quickly get the sort of results we'd really like, we're going to have to make a few changes to the limiters presented in the green bar at the top of the page. Our options are:

▶ **Results type:** Here you can choose from patents and articles, only articles, or legal opinions with a few different suboptions. We'll choose articles only.

▶ **Date:** The default is "anytime." Because our event in question occurred in early 2011, "since 2011" would be the best option for us.

▶ **Citations:** At the moment, this isn't necessarily relevant to our search, but you can choose to include articles with citations or just articles that include summaries but not necessarily include citations. We'll leave this at the default.

Figure 5.3 shows our revised search results.

Beyond limiting all results to scholarly content, Google Scholar offers some significantly different information about each result. For each result, if available, the following information will be presented:

▶ The title of the article will be linked to the primary source of the article along with an indication of the format, for example, .pdf or .html.

▶ **Figure 5.3: Google Scholar 2011 Article Results for "2011 japan tsunami"**

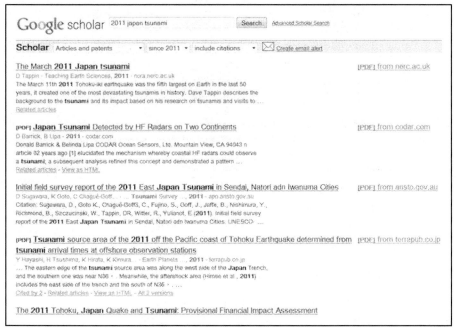

- The author(s) of the article, the publication year, and the domain name of the publication's website are listed.
- A brief abstract of the article will include your keywords in bold.
- The number of times the article has been cited by others is noted, with a link to a page of links to the articles containing those citations.
- Content originally presented as a PDF will have a link to an HTML version.

As you can see, these results, especially the citations, are specifically designed to be of use to scholars and researchers. There is one significant limitation in Google Scholar that you do need to be aware of. In some, if not many, cases, depending on your topic, the results may link to online database services such as Elsevier and Wilson that will charge you for access to the actual article. Not all of the results you'll find in Google Scholar will be free to access.

As with most other Google search services, Google Scholar has an advanced search option (http://scholar.google.com/advanced_scholar _search), designed, in this case, with the scholar in mind. At the top of the advanced search page are the standard Boolean operator fields followed by:

- **Author:** If you're looking for articles by a particular researcher, enter that information here.
- **Publication:** If you're looking for articles published in a particular journal, enter that here.
- **Date:** Unlike the date limiter on the search results page, here you can specify a range of years, for example, "2000–2002."
- **Collections:** Here you have more specific options than on the basic search results screen when it comes to limiting the type of sources you want. In our example, geology students can limit their search to the Biology, Life Sciences, and Environmental Science collection.

To see an example page, go to http://www.alatechsource.org/techset/semanticweb/ to access this figure: Google's Advanced Scholar Search Page

---

Now that we've found blogs about the tsunami and have some scholarly resources, let's take a look at how it was reported in the news. Instead of doing just a general news search, however, let's take a look at those results over time.

Visualizing via Google News Timeline

Many of you are probably already familiar with Google News (http://news .google.com/) where you can get the latest news headlines and search for online news content. However, over in Google Labs there is an alternative way to use Google News—the Google News Timeline (http://newstimeline .googlelabs.com/). Here you can perform the same searches as in Google News, but, instead of being presented a list of relevancy-ranked results, you'll be presented a timeline of results. Again, let's search for "2011 japan tsunami." Then, because "tsunami" can be used in other contexts as a metaphor and we know the date of the event (March 11, 2011), enter that in the date limiter at the top and change "Show:" to day instead of month.

To see our results, go to http://www.alatechsource.org/techset/semanticweb/ to access this figure: Google News Timeline for "2011 japan tsunami" for March 11, 2011

As you can quickly see, this is not your typical Google results list. Instead of a top-down list of results, now we're presented with the most relevant news results for each day in our timeline starting with the day of the event. Using the arrow buttons to the top-left and top-right of the timeline we can move our results display back and forward in time. Through such visualization we can quickly see the most relevant topics of the day (week, month, year, or decade) and see how the story developed over time.

Through the various options and limiters available on this page we can manipulate the type of results, the sources from which the results are found, and the display of those results. Let's run through these options:

- ▶ **News type:** To the left of the search box is a dropdown list that allows you to choose which type of news you're looking for. By default you're searching "News." Other options range from News Quotes, to News Photos, newspapers, magazines, blogs, and *Wikipedia*, to name a few.
- ▶ **Queries:** The first line at the top of our results currently tells us that we're displaying results from a general news search of "Japan Tsunami News" along with results from "Time Magazine" and "Wikipedia Events." Clicking the "x" icons to the right of any of these we can turn these results off. Additionally, we can click the "Add More Queries" link to add additional news sources to our timeline. Just keep in mind that the more sources you add, the more crowded the timeline will be.
- ▶ **Show:** Here you can change the timeline's scale between Day, Week, Month, Year, and Decade.
- ▶ **Size:** Choosing Small, Medium, or Large will change the size of the box of each result. As you add more queries, you may want to reduce the box size to be able to see all of the results. Increasing the box size will increase the amount of information displayed from each result.

> ► **Date:** The date entered here will establish the first date used for results and the first date displayed in the timeline. Click the "Go" button to set the timeline start to your date. You can always use the navigation buttons to move forward or backward from that date.
> ► **This Week:** When clicked this button will reset your time to begin on the Sunday of the current week.
> ► **Link:** Clicking "Link" will display the URL that when used will get you back to the timeline as you are currently viewing it. This allows you, or someone else, to view the timeline as you're currently seeing it.

Here's an important piece of advice about using the Google News Timeline. It is designed to dynamically update as you change the options. Therefore, *do not* use the back button in your browser while using this service. If you do, you'll go back to the original search page, and you will have lost any customizations that you made to your timeline. You have been warned.

Now that we've spent some time using some of Google's alternative search interfaces, let's take a look at some of the alternatives Bing has to offer.

Bing Social

While we were writing this chapter there was news of a bombing in Oslo, Norway, and then the next day there was a series of shootings at Utøya, Norway. Given that news was still breaking regarding these events and that there was significant worldwide public reaction, these were the sort of events that might lead you to want to see what people were saying online about them and to find out what links were being shared among those discussing the events. This is where Bing Social shines.

Bing Social (http://www.bing.com/social) allows you to search the contents of both Twitter and Facebook, which by itself isn't all that impressive. What makes Bing Social much more useful than just searching each of these sites individually is in how it presents the results. To best walk you through the results, let's first do a search for "oslo shooting." Figure 5.4 shows our results.

As you can see, the results are broken down into two parts: Shared Links and Public Updates. The Shared Links section is a list of links that are being shared by users on both Twitter and Facebook. This shows which sites related to your search people are sharing with their friends. The more the link has been shared, the more likely it is to appear on the list.

The Public Updates results are made up of actual Twitter and Facebook posts that mention your search terms. Here results are displayed in chronological order (newest on the top) and are updated in real time. This way, for active events, you can watch how people are talking about it on these services.

▶ **Figure 5.4: Bing Social Search Results for "oslo shooting"**

You can stop and start the real-time updating of the results using the play/pause icon to the right of these results.

You can get further and more detailed results for each of these result types by clicking on "Public Updates" or "Shared Links" at the top of the results page. On the Public Updates page, you'll continue to receive the real-time updates of your search along with the play/pause option, but in addition you can switch the results between "Most Recent" (the default) and "Best Match," which will provide relevancy-ranked results as opposed to time-based results.

To see our results, go to http://www.alatechsource.org/techset/semanticweb/ to access this figure: Bing Social Public Updates Search Results for "oslo shooting"

If you're more interested in the links being shared, switch to the Shared Links page. Here you'll get more results along with either the first tweet that shared the link or the number of Facebook users who have shared the link, as well as how long ago it was first shared, the URL of the link, which service it's being shared on, and how many times the link has been shared. Note that shared links are not updated in real time.

To see our results, go to http://www.alatechsource.org/techset/semanticweb/ to access this figure: Bing Social Shared Links Search Results for "oslo shooting"

Silobreaker

Earlier we looked at Google News Timeline for searching for news reporting on a historical event. Now let's take a look at Silobreaker (http://www.silo breaker.com/), continuing to use our more "current" event of the tragedies in Norway. Silobreaker has many different focuses, including news, financial, and entertainment, all of which are designed to "aggregate, analyze, contextualize and bring meaning to the ever-increasing amount of digital information." Given the example we're working with, we're going to focus on the news search. To get started, we'll use "oslo shooting" again.

To see our results, go to http://www.alatechsource.org/techset/semanticweb/ to access this figure: Silobreaker Results for "oslo news"

The page shows what the site describes as the results of the "360° Search." Here we're presented not with a typical list of linked web results but more of a newspaper-type display. The bars near the top of the page provide context for searches (in this case, "Global Issues | Conflicts & Crime"); then are listed news articles with headlines and images, along with when they were first reported, when they were last updated, number of related documents, entities (related keywords), and the source.

Further down the page is a list of real-time results from Twitter. Then come a relevant quote and a list of linked documents relevant to the search.

On the right side of the page are sections for videos. These are followed by "In focus" (as you hover over each item you'll receive additional information about that topic, location, or person); "Network," "Hot Spots," and "Trends" (each of which we'll look at in more detail); a list of related blog posts you can sort by date or relevance; and, finally, links to more audio and video content also sortable by date or relevance.

As great as all of this information is, the Network view of your search results (click "Network") will knock Silobreaker up into the next stage of search results by visualizing the connections among all of the discrete entities shown in the basic search results. Note all of the connections that have been drawn among the different companies, organizations, people, cities, key phrases, and products involved in this story.

To see our results, go to http://www.alatechsource.org/techset/semanticweb/ to access this figure: Silobreaker's Network Map for "oslo shooting"

Each entity is represented by a different icon. Hover over an icon, and the connections between it and the other entities will be highlighted. Hover over a connection point, and the connected entities will be highlighted. Hover over an entity name, and you'll be presented with a box of additional information about that item. If the map is too dense for you, you can grab and drag any item around to realign the lines to make them easier for you to view.

You can further customize the map by adjusting the sliders above the map. For example, if you're more interested in the people and organizations involved, use the organization and person sliders to increase the number of them displayed; reduce the number of other categories displayed by adjusting their sliders down.

If you're putting together a webpage of resources about this topic for your library's website, you can grab the HTML necessary for embedding the map into your site by clicking on the "Embed This" link below the map.

Next, let's take a look at the Hot Spots page for our search, which can be accessed at the top of the page above the search box. Here you'll be shown a Google map with cities mentioned in the search results highlighted. The bigger the red dot, the more important the location to the search. Beyond all the typical options you have with any Google map (panning, zooming, layers, etc.) you're also given date options at the bottom of the map. Here you can change the map to highlight the latest, past seven days', or past 30 days' locations or specify a date range you would like to use.

To see our results, go to http://www.alatechsource.org/techset/semanticweb/ to access this figure: Silobreaker Hot Spots Results for "oslo shooting"

Finally, let's explore the Trends view. This results view works best for search terms that encompass a longer time span. Because at the time of this writing our example story was so new, we'll use a different search to illustrate the use of Silobreaker's trends. Search for "barack obama."

To see our results, go to http://www.alatechsource.org/techset/semanticweb/ to access this figure: Silobreaker Trends Results for "barack obama"

The information presented in Trends is simple yet, depending on what you're researching, may be significant. What you see in Trends is the article volume for your search term over time. Silobreaker also added two additional lines relevant to our Obama search, in this case for John Boehner and Mitt Romney, to which we can compare the article volume. At this point you can add or remove terms and change the timescale to get the graph you're looking for.

Going back to our original example, create a Trends chart for "japan tsunami" for the past six months. To do this, type "japan" into the search box on the Trends page and select the suggested "Japan Earthquake & Tsunami [Keyphrase]" as your search term. Click "Search Trends," and, once you have the results, use the buttons below the chart to change the time frame to "6 months."

▶ SEARCH FOR REUSABLE ONLINE CONTENT

There are times when you, your coworkers, or one of your patrons will look for online content to reuse or repurpose. For example, your library's marketing department may want a great image that perfectly fits in with the library's latest campaign. A student will come into the library looking for an image or video to include in a school report that illustrates different kinds of snakes. There are countless reasons why you will need to find some online content that you can reuse. The trouble with this is the thorny issue of copyright.

Copyright Issues and Creative Commons

In the United States, anything created after 1972 is automatically granted copyright protection, even if the © symbol does not appear anywhere on, or in association with, the item. Content created prior to 1972 may or may not currently be covered under copyright. Content created prior to 1923 is generally considered now in the public domain. However, you must also consider the concept of fair use in which, under certain circumstances, copyrighted content can be reused. U.S. copyright law defines "fair use," but some content creators have a more liberal interpretation of what's considered fair use. Copyright is difficult to understand, and in some cases you may want to consult a lawyer to determine whether you can legally reuse content without permission.

Fortunately, the creation of Creative Commons licenses (http://www.creativecommons.org/) has resulted in a large amount of professional-grade content available online for others to reuse without needing to go through all of the hassles involved with getting permission under copyright or fearing they have violated the law. First, let's take a look at the basics of Creative Commons; then we'll show you some ways to find such content. At the end, we'll look at some sources for public domain content should you be in need of (generally) older content.

Creative Commons (CC) is a nonprofit organization, founded more than a decade ago, that provides licenses to content creators who are interested in giving certain permissions regarding their creations that are broader than those offered under U.S. copyright law. For example, Michael is an amateur photographer and posts nearly all of his photographs to his Flickr account (http://www.flickr.com/photos/travelinlibrarian/). Of course, Michael would prefer that someone who reuses one of his photos would pay him for the privilege, but he understands that many can't or won't do so. He would also prefer that, should someone wish to reuse one of his photos yet not pay, he at least gets credit for taking the photo in the first place. This is why most of his photos are licensed under the CC "attribution, non-commercial" license. This means that anyone is free to reuse a photo as long as Michael is given appropriate credit (usually in the form of a link back to the original photo's page in Flickr) and that the photo is used only in a noncommercial way. If you follow these rules, you're free to use the photo without first asking Michael for permission or paying him. If you're a commercial entity wishing to use the photo in a profit-making endeavor, such as printing the image in a magazine or in an advertisement, traditional copyright then comes into play, and you need to discuss terms with Michael.

There are other versions of a Creative Commons license. For example, Michael could license his photo as "attribution only," which means commercial use is okay, but he must be given credit. A "share alike" license means that anyone who reuses such content must also reshare their content under a similar license. All the types of licenses are defined at http://creativecommons.org/licenses/.

So, instead of taking the time to teach all of your patrons the ins and outs of copyright (which is a noble goal but good luck pulling it off), why not just encourage them to look for content for which permission to reuse is already given? Here's a few ways in which you can do just that.

Photographs

People are constantly looking for images that they can reuse. Whether it's for a promotional sign in the library, a photo for a presentation, or just a funny photo to include in a blog post, a photograph makes text more interesting. So, how can we find great photos online that are CC licensed?

The single largest online collection of photographs is Flickr's. Flickr contains tens of millions of photos from hundreds of thousands of photographers from around the world. Photographers range from award-winning professionals to your neighbor with his phone's built-in camera, and quality ranges from stellar to just plain bad. But, many of those photos have been licensed for you to reuse; because libraries are generally in the nonprofit sector, pretty much any CC-licensed photograph might cover what you want to do.

Flickr provides the option to limit your searches to CC-licensed content. You can find this at the bottom of the advanced search page (http://www .flickr.com/search/advanced/) in a section labeled "Creative Commons." This is a perfectly functional way to search for such content in Flickr, but there is a much better tool out there that we'd like to show you: Compfight.

Compfight (http://compfight.com/) does the same thing that the Flickr search option does but does it much more elegantly, and it is much easier to use. Type your search terms into the search box on Compfight's homepage, and click the search icon. For example, let's say we're looking for a photo of a confused person for a sign promoting the library's help desk. Type in "confused."

We'll get a lot of pretty good results, some of which might just work well for our sign. However, we're currently seeing results from Flickr regardless of the license attached to the photo. Some photos may be under traditional copyright and might not be available to us without sending some e-mails asking for permission.

On the left side of the screen, note that "Any license" is bold. Two other choices are "Creative Commons" and "Commercial." "Creative Commons" will limit our results to CC licensed but not for commercial use. "Commercial" will limit the results to CC licensed but licensed only for commercial use. Generally, the commercial option will provide us with fewer results, so click the "Creative Commons" link. Figure 5.5 shows the results.

Each photo is a link back to the original photo on Flickr.com from where you can verify which license is associated with the image and download the size appropriate for your project. Just be sure that whenever you do reuse a photo provide either a link back to, or the URL of, the original photo's Flickr page. Including the name of the photographer is also appreciated.

Video

Perhaps you're looking for a great video to go along with a blog post about the history of libraries. In most cases you would search for "libraries" on

▶ **Figure 5.5: Compfight CC-Licensed Results for "confused"**

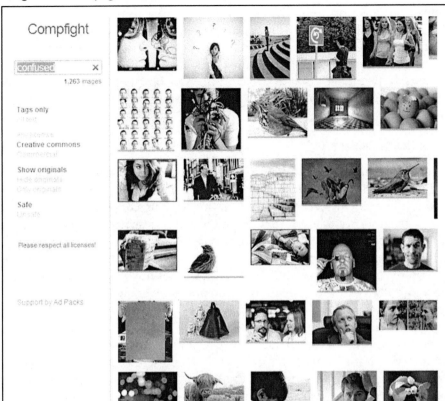

YouTube, find an appropriate video, and embed it into your blog post. The trouble with this is that the video you embed might not have been legally posted to YouTube in the first place. Should that video end up being caught and removed from YouTube, the copy you embedded into your blog post will also disappear.

To reduce the possibility of this happening, use only CC-licensed videos. First, search YouTube for your keyword(s), in this case, "library." Then, on the results page, click the "Filter & Explore" link in the upper left, and from there select "Creative Commons."

To see our results, along with the menu of options under "Filter & Explore," go to http:// www.alatechsource.org/techset/semanticweb/ to access this figure: Limiting to CC-Licensed Content in YouTube

The second result, "LIBRARY OF CONGRESS," looks like a good choice. Click on that to bring up the video. In this case, we've found a great old government video about the importance of the Library of Congress. It's a bit long, at 20 minutes, but it would still make a great addition to the blog post. So, open up the full video description, verify that it is licensed under CC, and then grab the embed code to place it into your blog post. The embed code will automatically provide a link back to the YouTube page, along with the necessary attribution.

Other Online Content

What about all of the other possible CC-licensed content that might be available online but not hosted on Flickr or YouTube? There are several ways to find this content. Let's take a look at one: finding content via Google.

For example, a student comes to the reference desk needing assistance on a report about snakes. She wants some images and maybe a video or two but also some text-based content to reuse—and maybe more than what might be considered generally okay within the bounds of fair use. Because we're looking for more than just one specific type of content, Google is a better place to start than Flickr or YouTube. Google is also CC-license aware and allows us to limit our results to just this sort of content.

To find these options, head over to Google's Advanced Search screen (http://www.google.com/advanced_search), and scroll down to and click on "+Date, usage rights, region, and more." This will extend the advanced search screen, adding such options as date, keyword location, and numeric limiters. In our case, we want the "Usage rights" limiter. Fill in all of your other options accordingly, choose "Free to use or share" under usage rights, and click the search button. (Because we're dealing with a student, we've also set the reading level option to "annotate results with reading levels" to help us find the correct level of content for our patron.) Figure 5.6 shows the results.

Google indicates that all of the results listed are "free to use or share." Results range from *Wikipedia* articles to images to other websites about snakes. Other related Google search types are listed on the left (images, news, videos, etc.); these can be used to further limit the results, all of which will continue to provide CC-licensed content until we choose to turn that limiter back off.

The Public Domain

Although searching for CC-licensed content is a great way to find easily reusable online content, there is also a large amount of public domain content

▶ Figure 5.6: CC-Licensed Google Search Results

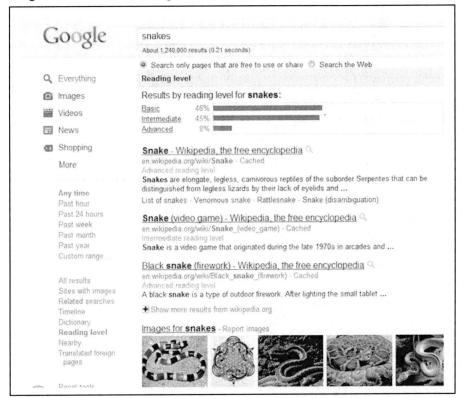

available online. Content in the public domain means that it is no longer, or never was, under the realm of copyright and is currently free for anyone to use under any circumstances. However, this is still an area that can be fraught with some confusion, as someone may think that something is in the public domain even though it is not. The first thing to do is determine if something is in the public domain before using it, typically by seeing if the content in some way explicitly states that it is public domain content.

The largest collection of public domain material online is in the Internet Archive (http://www.archive.org/). The Internet Archive contains a vast amount of material ranging from audio to video to full digital version of books. It also contains archived versions of an amazing number of webpages, which are accessible via its Wayback Machine (http://wayback.archive.org/web/). The majority of the Archive's content is either CC licensed or in the public domain. (However, note that the content of the Wayback Machine is still covered by traditional copyright unless the pages being archived expressly state otherwise.)

In most cases you can simply search the Internet Archive's content and verify the item's license on the item's page. Because most of the content is free to use, this will serve most users' purposes. However, let's say, for example, that your patron is looking for public domain audio regarding World War II. In this case, you'll need to use the Advanced Search page (http://www .archive.org/advancedsearch.php) and fill in the following fields:

- Any field: contains *wwii*
- AND Mediatype: *is audio*
- AND *license* contains *publicdomain*

The results of this search range from lectures regarding music from World War II to recordings of Nazi propaganda broadcasts, all ready to be downloaded and used by your patron.

To see our results, go to http://www.alatechsource.org/techset/semanticweb/ to access this figure: Internet Archive Public Domain Search Results

---

▶ EXPLORE DATA AND STATISTICS THROUGH WOLFRAMALPHA

WolframAlpha (http://www.wolframalpha.com/) isn't a search engine. Well, it's not a search engine as we're used to thinking of them. Although it does perform searches on your behalf, it doesn't search the web; it searches an immense collection of available online data, including mathematical, scientific, and statistical data, such as population and weather-related data.

WolframAlpha bills itself not as a search engine but as a "computational knowledge engine." According to its homepage, WolframAlpha allows you to "answer questions; do math; instantly get facts, calculators, unit conversions, and real-time quantitative data and statistics; create plots and visualizations; and access vast scientific, technical, chemical, medical, health, business, financial, weather, geographic, dictionary, calendar, reference, and general knowledge—and much more." Basically, if what you're looking for is data, this might be just the best place to start.

The best way to wrap your mind around what WolframAlpha offers and can do is to play around with it. When it comes to applications in the library world, the most direct would be at the reference desk and for academic librarians who provide direct research assistance in the math- and science-related fields. Because we can't assume that you, the reader (or the authors, for that matter) have any significant math or science background, let's use homicide rates as our basis for working with WolframAlpha.

Accessing and Comparing Data

WolframAlpha is designed to be searched using natural language queries. In other words, you just ask it a question; there's no syntax that you need to learn. So, let's say that a patron is doing some research into homicide rates in Nebraska and would like to start with the state's capitol, Lincoln. Type in the following question: "what is the homicide rate in lincoln, ne?"

Instead of providing a list of links to webpages that contain the keywords you typed in, many of which would contain the general answer you're looking for, WolframAlpha distinguishes itself from sites like Google and Bing immediately.

To see the complete results for this question, go to http://www.alatechsource.org/techset/ semanticweb/ to access this figure: WolframAlpha Results for "what is the homicide rate in lincoln, ne?"

Looking down this page, you'll first see the "Input interpretation." These are the significant keywords that were pulled out of your question upon which WolframAlpha based its results. (Once you get the hang of it you'll realize that you can just type in these words instead of typing in a full question.) Next, in "Result," it presents data that it feels is most relevant to your query (here, it is the number of this type of crime per 100,000 people in 2008). Then it gives the Nebraska average compared to the national average, a chart of the data over time followed, and then statistics for the area's overall crime and other violent crime rates. Try getting all this from Google in a single search.

Now let's take this to the next level. Remember, WolframAlpha bills itself as being able to do computations and comparisons. Let's change our question a bit: "what is the homicide rate in lincoln, ne vs omaha?"

To see our results, go to http://www.alatechsource.org/techset/semanticweb/ to access this figure: WolframAlpha Results for "what is the homicide rate in lincoln, ne vs omaha?"

We're now asking for information about the homicide rate in two locations, and WolframAlpha is able to present the data from both locations in relationship to each other. Each of the charts of data provided contact two sets of data points, allowing us to easily compare the results side by side.

Each section has options for changing various options, such as scale and time period (linear scale versus log scale or the unit of measurement, for example). Some sections have a more/less option to add or remove available data from the results page, and some have a "Show Chart" to display tabled data as a bar chart. All of the presented data can also be downloaded as a PDF or as a data file for use with the program Mathematica (http://www.wolfram.com/mathematica/) for those who wish to view and manipulate the data independently. Finally, a "Source information" link at the bottom of the page will provide a list of the sources for all of the data on the page.

Needless to say, WolframAlpha can do much more than just present and compare crime statistics. Topics include mathematics, statistical analysis, physics, health and medicine, chemistry, weather, and astronomy, to name a few. A complete directory of topics and links to many examples can be found at http://www.wolframalpha.com/examples/.

WolframAlpha Widgets

Another way that a library can leverage WolframAlpha's amazing data repository is through its widgets (http://www.wolframalpha.com/widgets/). With these customizable pieces of code, you can develop interactive pages on your websites to provide direct access to WolframAlpha's data and abilities. Providing a walkthrough of how to build your own widgets from scratch would take a chapter by itself; instead, let's look in the Widget Gallery (http://www.wolframalpha.com/widgets/gallery/) to find one that's been created. From there we'll show you the basic steps necessary to get one to appear on your library's site.

Let's say that you're an academic librarian and that your campus has a strong economics department. As such, you consistently encounter freshman economic majors looking for data comparing two states on, for example, such items as GDP, housing starts, and unemployment rates. For just such a question the WolframAlpha user C. Alan Joyce has built the "US State Economic Comparisons" widget (http://www.wolframalpha.com/widgets/view.jsp?id=1e20930364da4f6f53f118467c2648b9). Because this is the sort of question you get regularly, embedding this widget into your website would serve two purposes. First, staff would have an easy tool with which to answer this question. Second, you could offer patrons access to the same tool, thus saving staff time for other questions. On this page, you can test the widget, perform some basic customizations on the widget, and get the code needed to embed it within your webpage.

To see this page, go to http://www.alatechsource.org/techset/semanticweb/ to access this figure: The WolframAlpha "US State Economic Comparisons" Widget

---

The first step is to test the widget to make sure it performs the computations you need. In this case, choose one of the comparison types (GDP, housing starts, housing permits, tax collections, or unemployment), and enter the two states you'd like to compare. Click "Submit" to run the comparison. Close the results window to return to the widget.

To see our results, go to http://www.alatechsource.org/techset/semanticweb/ to access this figure: The WolframAlpha "US State Economic Comparisons" Results

---

The next step is to customize the widgets to best fit your needs. Unless you are building your own widget from scratch there aren't a lot of options, but they are useful. First, you have several colors to choose from to match the widget to your website's design. Next, you can choose from three output designs: Lightbox, Popup, and Inline. These control the style of the results display. Then you can set the dimensions (in pixels) of the output display. In each case, the test widget will adjust to your new settings, giving you a preview of what your users will see on your site.

The final step is to copy the appropriate embedding HTML code and paste it into the place on your website where you want it to appear. Code is available for several different platforms, such as Blogger, WordPress, and iGoogle. If you're embedding it in a library website not on one of these platforms, you'll want the default HTML code indicated by the </> icon.

▶ CREATE SEARCHABLE METADATA IN FLICKR

Given the future potential of the Semantic Web, many Semantic Web projects are in their infancy. However, there are projects that libraries can do now that will enrich their data, making it easier to find now and laying the groundwork for the semantic search tools yet to come. Many libraries already use Flickr to store, share, and host their photos or videos and images, because Flickr provides easy-to-use guided metadata creation. In fact, if you use Flickr at all, you have probably already created metadata without even thinking about it! In this section, we will explore the world of adding metadata to images via Flickr (http://www.flickr.com/), a robust image hosting and community site.

Creating metadata in Flickr is a painless task that can not only be fun but also a community event itself (see yourself in a photo or video? recognize the location? tag them!). Having good metadata for image collections makes them more searchable, more harvestable by search engines, and even sub-scribable via an RSS reader—in other words, users can subscribe to your images! Tagging uploaded photos or videos from an event such as a book club meeting means that users can easily find and see all of your images for the book club meetings. Additionally, there are third-party applications to create slide shows and other nifty tools for your website—many of which use tags to group items.

Flickr is a popular image sharing site owned by Yahoo! and has been used by librarians for many years as a means of displaying photos (and, more recently, short videos) on, and archiving to, the web. Libraries have also used Flickr to tap into social media by creating scavenger hunts, daily photos, or video collages and to seek assistance in identifying unknown people in photos or videos. Much of the metadata created in Flickr is indexed and searchable through Google Images (http://images.google.com/), Bing Images (http://www.bing.com/images), and of course Yahoo! Images (http://images.search.yahoo.com/). Video metadata is slowly becoming harvestable and will continue to be created as more content moves to multimedia. Flickr makes sharing photos and videos easy and fun—so why not provide a little more information and ensure that your users and community find *your* images?

Why Use Flickr?

Flickr offers many advantages for image sharing over just uploading them to a folder on your web server. It provides an easy way to post your images that allows for sharing, embedding into other websites, commenting, tagging, view tracking, and, most relevant to this discussion, enhancement via metadata. Although free to get started, at some point you will likely want to purchase the relatively inexpensive ($25/year) Pro account, which provides much more storage space, organizational features, and other perks (see http://www. flickr.com/upgrade/ for a brief overview of the features of the Pro account). Free accounts allow you to store only 200 images at any one time. Paid accounts, on the other hand, allow an unlimited number.

Flickr also provides some basic image editing features (along with additional features via the Picnik service), the ability to easily assign copyright, and the ability to share across a community and publish on other social media sites. One of the key advantages of Flickr in terms of metadata is that it will harvest some information from your camera, such as the date taken, type of camera, and type of file format. This harvested data is called EXIF (EXchangeable Image File format) and is actually embedded into the data bits of .jpg image files, a common format used by digital cameras. Assuming your camera supplies the EXIF data, you can see this harvested data at work in Flickr under the "View EXIF info" menu item. You will see a large amount of information about your photos, including but not limited to the date the photo or video was taken, type of camera used, ISO speed, DPI, exposure mode, and white balance setting. Although raw EXIF is generally not indexed via the common search engines such as Google, by using Flickr, much of that harvested metadata does become searchable in many ways.

In addition to the EXIF data, when you add a title, geotag (location information), or tags to photos or video in Flickr, you're creating descriptive metadata. When you put your images into a set or a group, you're also creating metadata. When you pick a usage license, you're assigning rights metadata. Flickr provides simple interfaces for creating metadata whether through form fields during the uploading process or through your ability to directly edit most information that is displayed on a photo or video page. You do not need to do any coding, and you do not need to know what the types of metadata are; you just fill in the information as you get to it. Other than the information that is uploaded along with the image file itself, Flickr doesn't require you to do anything in terms of metadata; it's all optional. However, the more metadata you add, the better the chances that you, or someone else, will be able to find your image at a later date.

Getting Started with Flickr

If you don't already have a Flickr account, the first thing you'll need to do is sign up for one. At this point there's no need to get a Pro account unless you're ready to upload more than 200 images. You can set up a new account by connecting it to an existing Facebook, Google, or Yahoo! account or create a new account from scratch. Each of these methods has its own benefits, so we'll leave that up to you. Whether your Flickr account is for personal use or for the library isn't relevant for this exercise. Once you have created a log-in, you will probably want to configure your account settings (click "You" and then "Your Account").

These settings will impact what default metadata (such as rights) is applied to your images; additionally, they will set whether your content is private or publicly available. Another setting that you will need to decide on is whether you will allow import of EXIF metadata for location for your photographs. This feature allows Flickr to get the location of where the photo was taken, if your camera records that information. If you are using a DSLR (Digital Single-Reflex Lens or digital SLR) like the Canon Rebel, a webcam, or mobile device, you most likely have GPS and location, but you will need to make sure that the GPS/location setting is turned on when you are using your device to take photos. Regardless of what you choose for your account settings, you can override or change information for specific images; in other words, you can set your account to public but then make some images private. You can also change the rights of usage on individual photos or videos and change or hide the location information.

Uploading and Tagging Your Photos or Videos

Once logged in, to upload images, click on the "Upload" link in the menu across the top of any Flickr page. By default, you'll be offered a flash-based interface that allows you to batch upload a group of files. You can also select the "basic uploader," which allows you to upload up to six individual files. (You would also use this option if the computer you are using does not have Adobe Flash installed.)

Upon uploading images, Flickr not only harvests what metadata it can from the uploaded file itself but also guides you through adding metadata during the upload process. If you batch upload, Flickr will prompt you to add titles and tags after the upload process is complete. If you upload individually, you will be offered the option to add some metadata prior to the actual uploading. No matter which process you use, you can always add, remove, and edit metadata at a later time. So, you will log in, upload photos or videos, fill in all of the information that Flickr asks for during the upload process, including tags, titles, and descriptions, and add your images to a set (a collection or album) if you desire. Flickr will apply your default information as set in your account settings.

Once you have uploaded your photos, you may find that you need to tweak them slightly. Perhaps you want to limit downloading of images, which you can do by choosing "All Rights Reserved" in the rights field. This and other information can be edited through the image's individual page by clicking in the appropriate field or in the description. Other types of editable metadata on its page will be hyperlinked guided text ("add a person," "add a tag," etc.). You can also use the batch organizer (click "You" and then "Organize & Create") to make changes to groups of photos or videos. You can even mix videos and photos together for batch editing of metadata! For example, if you have a large quantity of photos and a few videos from the book club meeting, you may want to batch upload them and then do the metadata work in bulk, saving typing and time.

Adding Metadata

Whether you upload images individually or in groups, you will have a number of metadata options. The standard photos or video uploader is a guided process via a flash-based interface. You choose your images and upload them; batch uploads will bring up the organizer so that you can easily do multiple edits. In the standard uploader, some of the metadata features are accessed by the "Show advanced settings..." link.

The filename will become the title of the photo or video. Additionally, your account settings will apply its defaults, such as rights statements, if you do not choose otherwise. These options are also available through the basic uploader, a single upload process for both batch and single uploads, with all metadata fields on one screen:

▶ **Add tags:** The keywords you enter here, as a comma-delimited list, are added to all of the images that you upload via this screen. In general, the more tags the better, as they all become searchable metadata and increase the likelihood that someone will find your photos or video. You can also use these tags later to find particular photos or videos to create a slide show or sets.

▶ **Choose the privacy settings:** Here you choose who can see the photos or videos—only you, your Flickr "friends," your Flickr "family," or anyone, Flickr account holder or not (public). You can also set a default via your Flickr profile so that you don't have to worry about this option every time you upload images.

▶ **Set safety level:** Flickr has a built-in "adult" filter and assumes that your images do not contain "adult" content. This is the default "Safe" setting for uploaded images. Should your content contain racy content or nudity, we highly suggest you set the safety level of your images appropriately. Higher levels will restrict the types of users or nonusers that can see your content. Failure to set the safety level appropriately is a violation of Flickr's terms of service and can result in the closing of your account.

▶ **Set content type:** Flickr also likes to know what type of images you're uploading. By default it assumes you are uploading photos and/or videos. Here you can also indicate that your content is either screenshots or other nonphotographic content. However, even though these file types are allowed, Flickr's terms of service do indicate that the majority of your content should be photographs.

▶ **Hide these images from public searches:** You can check this option to keep your images from appearing as search results. However, you probably don't want to do this, as it defeats the purpose of adding metadata.

Tip

By default, the title of your image will be taken from the filename of the image sans the file extension. We highly recommend that, before uploading your images, you take the time to change the filenames from something like "D3467982.JPG" to something more appropriate, such as "Library Director Lisa Smith.jpg."

When you have finished uploading your photographs, you have the following choices:

▶ **Add to a Set/Create a new set...:** One of the more popular features of Flickr is the ability to organize images into sets. Each set contains multiple images from a single user usually grouped around a single event or theme. Here you can choose to add your newly uploaded images into an existing set in your account or create a new set to contain these images.

▶ **Title:** Here you can edit the title for each image. As mentioned previously, the default title is taken from the uploaded image's filename. The more descriptive the title, the more findable your image will be.

▶ **Description:** Here you can add a long-form description of your image. For example, the title may be "Library Director Lisa Smith," but the description might include a brief biography and/or contact information. A photo or video of an event might have the title of the event, and the description could contain information about when and where the event was held. All content of the description is searchable.

▶ **Tags:** Here you can edit the tags for individual photos or videos.

Editing Metadata for an Existing Image

Opening the page for a particular image allows you to edit any of the editable metadata for that image. For example, if during the upload process you forgot to add a tag to one image, click the "add a tag" link on the page. Conversely, if the image has an incorrect tag, click the "x" next to that tag to remove it. You can also click on the image's title and description to edit those, move photos or video to a set or a group, and identify individuals within the photos or video. Finally, you can also change the license and privacy settings for the images.

The Actions menu on this page provides even more options, including the ability to edit the image itself, view the EXIF data, replace a photo or video with a new version, add notes, add to a map, order prints, and further edit all of the other information we described in the previous paragraph.

The Organizer—Batch Metadata Editing

Clicking the "Organize & Create" link in the menu at the top of any Flickr page takes you to the Organizer, which provides very detailed and advanced metadata that you can batch edit. The first step is to select the images from your account that you wish to edit. This can be done by scrolling through the images at the bottom of the page or by searching within your account. Once you have found the images you wish to edit, drag them from the bottom of the screen into the larger editing area in the middle of the screen. Now you're ready to work with the following features:

▶ **Edit Photos or Videos:** Titles, Tags, Descriptions; Rotate (image editing); Delete

▶ **Permissions:** Privacy, Commenting, Tagging; Content Type, and Indexing (whether it can be found in a search)

▶ **Edit Dates**

▶ **Add People** (tag people)

▶ **Add Tags** (keywords)

▶ **Add to Group** (Flickr group, like a community album)

▶ **Locations:** Change location, add/remove from map

Other options include Print and Create (create photography projects like scrapbooks and calendars), Groups, and adding links to your photos or videostream (your photos or videos arranged chronologically).

Adding Location Data to Flickr

If your webcam, DSLR, or cell phone records your location, you can automatically load your photo's location during the upload process. Location metadata is embedded into the EXIF for your image. To make sure that Flickr can read your location information, you will need to check your Account Settings. Under You > Your Account > Privacy and Permissions, check "Import EXIF location data" to allow Flickr to read your location information. Additional settings for location that can impact how you share and display location data include the options for "Who will be able to see your stuff on a map" and "Hide your EXIF data." For each of these options you can choose to set it to only you, to groups of people (such as friends, contacts, family), or to everyone. "Hide your EXIF data" will hide not only your location but also the date the photo or video was taken as well as the type of camera. These two settings can also be tweaked later, unlike the "Import EXIF location data." If this option is turned off, your only way to enter location data is manually. Of course, not all devices will share location data, so Flickr has many tools to add location metadata (geometadata). Figure 5.7 shows one way that Flickr uses location metadata.

You can edit the location data through the image's individual page using the Batch Organizer or using Your Map. On the "Map" tab, which appears as "Your Map" under "Organize & Create" or adjacent to the "Batch Organizer" tab, you can drag and drop your photos or videos directly onto a map. If your scale is too small, Flickr will ask you if you want to zoom in to create accuracy (which in turn creates better metadata). Flickr will then create the geometadata for you (longitude and latitude). Another way to edit location is through the Batch Organizer. After you pull images to your workspace, you can edit the geometadata after clicking the "Location" tab. There you can

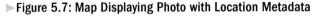

Figure 5.7: Map Displaying Photo with Location Metadata

change who can see the location assigned to your photos or video (Location > Change geoprivacy), add your photos or video to the Map (Location > Add items to the map), or remove your photos or video from the Map (Location > Remove items from the map).

Another option is to add location metadata directly on the image's page. If your image has no location metadata, you will see a map with the blurb "Add this photo or video to your map." You can also edit geometadata on the individual page, too. If you have added geometadata you will see it displayed under information about your camera, for example, "this photo or video was taken on June 2, 2011, in Atlanta, Georgia, using a Canon XSI camera." Clicking on the location (in this example, Atlanta) or on the location in the map snapshot below the text will bring up the map with your image and a link to edit the location. In that menu, you will see dropdowns of choices, including higher level (such as state) and city level (such as neighborhood).

Community and Flickr

As discussed, you can easily create sets of your images around an event or a theme. Michael, for example, has sets for each of the conferences he's attended (events) as well as sets for vanity license plates and limited edition books in his personal collection (themes). As great as sets are, they're not exactly community oriented, as each set may contain images from only one account. To join a larger Flickr community, you need to add photos or videos to a group.

One way to think of groups is as community photos or video albums through which photos or videos from multiple users are shared and a discussion may develop. Once a group is created, you can add your photos or videos to the group. You will always retain control over your image while also sharing it with a particular community. What may also happen is a group member may contact you requesting that a particular photo or video of yours be added to their group. For example, Michael takes a photo or video of an interesting sign in a library and posts it to his Flickr account. Later, an administrator of the group Library Signage (http://www.flickr.com/groups/librarysignage/) comments on his photo or video asking if he would add it to that group. Once Michael adds the image to the group the image appears in the group, yet he still retains the rights to, and control over, it. If he later deletes the image, it disappears from the group. Additionally, he can remove it from the group if he would like.

Flickr has been about community from the beginning, and there are many ways to share and connect with others via Flickr and images posted at Flickr. Each image has its own URL, which can be linked to from a website (provided the image is set to public), and most images can be embedded within another site. Sets, groups, your photos or videostream, individual tags, and even search results all have associated RSS feeds (and metadata!) that anyone can subscribe to. There are many interesting uses of Flickr, most of which are driven by metadata. So, get going! Reach out to those in your community to help you identify people and places in old photos or videos; create a digital scrapbook of your next event; or share floor maps or other library information in a visual format. You can do it all at Flickr, and, through creating the metadata, you enrich your photos and videos, making them more findable on the web.

▶ SEMANTICIZE SIMPLE DATA WITH GOOGLE'S RICH SNIPPETS

In this section we will explore how to semanticize webpages and websites. Semanticizing websites and pages just means that we massage the data and structure behind our websites and provide "hooks" so that the powerful search mechanisms (spiders and bots) of Google, Bing, and other search engines can successfully identify the content of our webpages instead of just performing straight keyword matches. The payoff for doing this can be enormous, such as providing more tailored content that can then lead to new services (such as automatically pushing library contact information to smartphones and mobile devices), a deeper searching experience, and the ability to search vertically through resources versus a wide shallow pass.

Google's Rich Snippets tool (http://www.google.com/support/webmasters/bin/answer.py?answer=99170) is one way of coding data that allows contextual information—such as parts of a book review, ingredients in a recipe, or the different parts of an address—to be embedded into websites, making for a more semantic and useful web experience. Rich snippets are just bits of metadata that help expose data to the web, making information more accessible to search engines, especially Google.

The Benefits of Rich Snippets

When you format your website content for rich snippets, you are creating enriched data that provides contextual information, which optimizes it for search engines and also makes it harvestable by mobile devices. Current uses of contextual information include linking reviews with services, building address books (both people information and organizational information), and publicizing events. Each of these types of contextual information follows a specific set of rules for coding that makes the data understandable to a search engine (kind of like road signs that tell drivers where to go and where to park). Rich snippets created with Google's tool are used by the Google search engine, making this enriched data available to a large group of searchers. Additionally, the format of this type of data (RDFa; microformats) is a Semantic Web standard and will potentially be harvestable by yet-to-be developed Semantic Web search tools.

Given that Google's Rich Snippets was introduced in 2009 and is just now expanding to include more contextual information, it is a truly cutting-edge technology, and few libraries have yet taken advantage of it. Both rich snippets and microformats (a set of "rules" for coding address book–like information) are just beginning to be utilized more broadly across the web. However, as the Semantic Web is becoming more prominent in the search landscape, a semantic markup tool like Google's Rich Snippets is a huge asset. Data from rich snippets is folded right into search results. With more and more search results, the ability to see contextual information can be a tremendous asset when searching.

Preparing Your Data with Google's Rich Snippets

In this project, we'll show you how to format some of your library's website content using Google's Rich Snippets so that your data will be more accessible, smarter, and even more portable! Enriching your metadata using Rich Snippets has two benefits: it helps to make your web content more semantic, especially to Google, which makes use of rich snippets, and it creates data that is readily available to mobile devices. Having a staff directory marked up with microformats (standard formats for address book–like information, such as name, address, and phone number) means that users can easily download information from your site into their phones and other mobile devices.

Google's Rich Snippets is not just a tool; it is also a way of using specific markup that Google recognizes, and it has the added benefit of working with standard rules for metadata used across the web and mobile devices at large. So, using Google's Rich Snippets will not only make your "Google-rich" content more accessible to Google, but it has the added bonus of being used in other search mechanisms, mobile devices, and apps. Google has yet to develop a tool (online or downloadable) to create metadata for rich snippets; however, there are tools out there to help you create metadata (such as microformat generators). Rich Snippets contains an introduction to rich snippets and metadata from a web editor's viewpoint as well as a metadata checking tool by website address (URL) to verify the structure of the metadata in terms of harvestability for Google's Rich Snippets. This way you can test out your snippets before adding them to your site.

Choosing Your Content

First, you need to decide what content you'll be contextualizing for the Semantic Web. The types of information appropriate for rich snippets include:

- ▶ Reviews and ratings (written descriptive reviews as well as ratings systems, e.g., 4 out of 5 stars; think book reviews, gift shop items, etc.—any service or item that can be assigned a rating)
- ▶ Directory and contact information (e.g., staff directory, general library contact info)
- ▶ Events (readings, special programming, art exhibits, storytime, etc.)
- ▶ Organization information

▶ Bread crumbs (navigational elements)
▶ Videos

For this discussion, we'll enrich data in a sample staff directory through marking up existing content. You will need to have some basic familiarity with HTML as well as with the tools to edit a live webpage. Sample code is available on the companion website (http://www.alatechsource.org/techset/ semanticweb/) or can be created following the guidelines we provide. If you are a more advanced user and wish to use an existing website, you can do that, too, but you may need to consult the Rich Snippets resources to mark up your specific page if it contains information beyond what is covered here (see Google's knol section on rich snippets at http://knol.google.com/k/ google-rich-snippets-tips-and-tricks for more details).

Getting Started

In this exercise we will enrich data in a sample staff directory. Rich snippets created with Google have several types of markup depending on the content type; for example, an address book would follow formatting guidelines for the "people" category, and a recipe would follow guidelines for the "recipes" category. Because we'll be working with a sample staff directory, we will follow the formatting guidelines for people (http://www.google.com/webmasters/ tools/richsnippets), which uses the hCard microformat, and we will use metadata standard microformats. Because microformats are accessible to mobile devices, a page that has been coded with microformats can load the information directly into your phone's address book. This way, your patrons can also add your semanticized data to their mobile phones with ease.

Creating a Sample to Work With

To start, we will create a simple staff directory that contains name, address, job title, organization, phone number, and e-mail address. Alternatively, if you have an existing directory you can use that (but you will need to have an understanding of how to work with your website's code).

Open your HTML editor and enter the following:

```
<!DOCTYPE html PUBLIC "-//W3C//DTD XHTML 1.0 Strict//EN"
  "http://www.w3.org/TR/xhtml1/DTD/xhtml1-strict.dtd">
<html xmlns="http://www.w3.org/1999/xhtml" lang="en" xml:
  lang="en">
<head>
<meta content="text/html; charset=iso-8859-1" http-equiv=
  "Content-Type" />
<title>Staff Directory</title>
</head>
```

```
<body>
<h1>Staff Directory</h1>
<div>
Name: Robin Fay<br />
Title: Information Professional<br />
Organization: UGA<br />
Address: Jackson St<br />
Athens, GA 30602<br />
US<br />
Email: <a href=mailto:georgiawebgurl@gmail.com>
  georgiawebgurl@gmail.com</a><br />
Phone: 000.000.0000
</div>
<div>
Name: Michael Sauers<br />
Title: Technology Innovation Librarian<br />
Organization: Nebraska Library Commission<br />
Address: The Atrium, 1200 N St., Suite 120<br />
Lincoln, NE 68508<br />
US<br />
Email: <a href=mailto:msauers@travelinlibrarian.info>
  msauers@travelinlibrarian.info</a><br />
Phone: 999.999.9999
</div>
</body>
</html>
```

Save your new file as staffdirectory.html (with no ending punctuation).

Right now this is just a basic HTML-formatted webpage containing contact information for two individuals. Next, we'll start to add additional code to give context to our content.

Formatting the Data

Now that we have the webpage staffdirectory.html we will add additional codes to the content that Google's Rich Snippets will then recognize as additional semantic information about our content. For our purposes, we will follow the formatting guidelines for people (http://www.google.com/ support/webmasters/bin/answer.py?answer=146646), which uses the hCard microformat. (To discover other formats and properties for other types of data, visit the Next Steps section of the Google Rich Snippets page, http:// www.google.com/support/webmasters/bin/answer.py?answer=99170.)

Table 5.1 lists the markup properties to use for each bit of information in your directory. (Which properties you use depends on what information

► Table 5.1: Markup for a Directory

Property	Description
name (fn)	Person's name (required)
nickname	Nickname
photo	Image link
title	Person's title (e.g., Financial Manager)
role	Person's role (e.g., Accountant)
url	Link to a webpage, such as the person's homepage
affiliation (org)	Name of an organization with which the person is associated (e.g., an employer) (If fn and org have the exact same value, Google will interpret the information as referring to a business or organization, not a person.)
friend	Identifies a social relationship between the person described and another person
contact	Identifies a social relationship between the person described and another person
acquaintance	Identifies a social relationship between the person described and another person
address (adr)	Location of the person (can have the subproperties street-address, locality, region, postal-code, and country-name)

your directory includes; you don't have to use them all.) The first property listed, name, is actually the RDFa tag, which is necessary; fn, in parentheses, is the tag for a microformat, which we are using.

Now, we want to start marking up our data with the properties defined by Google. Each of our data fields will be preceded by a respective microformat property. We will go line by line through the first entry. If you're using a blogging platform or another content management system, there are hCard and other microformat plug-ins available. However, as with most code-generating programs, you may need to tweak the output to get it to validate. Knowing how to edit the code is extremely helpful in troubleshooting!

According to the rules of the hCard microformat, the first thing we need to do is establish each individual hCard or person listed in our document. In our case we have two; the first starts on line 9 and the second on line 19. Let's just focus on Robin's information first. We need to update line 9 with the appropriate hCard code. Thus, this line now reads:

```
<div id="hcard-robin-fay" class="vcard">
Name: Robin Fay<br />
Title: Information Professional<br />
```

```
Organization: UGA<br />
Address: Jackson St<br />
Athens, GA 30602<br />
US<br />
Email: <a href=mailto:georgiawebgurl@gmail.com>georgia
    webgurl@gmail.com</a><br />
Phone: 000-000-0000
</div>
```

Next, we need to enclose Robin's information in the markup that indicates we're describing a person (along with a matching closing div):

```
<div id="hcard-robin-fay" class="vcard">
<div itemscope="" itemtype="http://data-vocabulary.org/
    Person">
Name: Robin Fay<br />
Title: Information Professional<br />
Organization: UGA<br />
Address: Jackson St<br />
Athens, GA 30602<br />
US<br />
Email: <a href=mailto:georgiawebgurl@gmail.com>
    georgiawebgurl@gmail.com</a><br />
Phone: 000-000-0000
</div>
</div>
```

What we now need to do is go through the rest of Robin's contact information and, using the markup specified in Table 5.1, match each of the appropriate properties to our content. As a result, Robin's information will end up coded as follows:

```
<div id="hcard-robin-fay" class="vcard">
<div itemscope="" itemtype="http://data-vocabulary
    .org/Person">
<span itemprop="name">Robin Fay</span>,
Name: <span class="fn">Robin Fay</span><br />
Title: <span itemprop="title">Information Professional
    </span><br />
Organization: <span itemprop="affiliation">UGA </span>.<br />
Address: <div class="adr">
    <span class="street-address">Jackson St</span><br />
    <span class="locality">Athens</span>
    <span class="region">GA</span>
    <span class="postal-code">30602</span><br />
    <span class="country-name">US</span><br />
```

```
Email: <a class="email" href="mailto:georgiawebgurl@
  gmail.com">
georgiawebgurl@gmail.com</a><br />
Telephone: <span class="tel">000-000-0000</span>
</div>
</div>
```

Now that you've seen how it was done for Robin, why don't you add the appropriate codes to Michael's contact information before looking at the result? (Remember, copy and paste is your friend.) Michael's information should look like this:

```
<div id="hcard-michael-sauers" class="vcard">
<div itemscope="" itemtype="http://data-vocabulary
  .org/ Person">
<span itemprop="name">Michael Sauers</span>,
Name: <span class="fn">Michael Sauers</span><br />
Title: <span itemprop="title">Technology Innovation
  Librarian </span><br />
Organization: <span itemprop="affiliation">Nebraska
  Library Commission</span>.<br />
Address: <div class="adr">
  <span class="street-address">The Atrium, 1200 N St,
Suite 120</span><br />
  <span class="locality">Lincoln</span>
  <span class="region">NE</span>
  <span class="postal-code">68508</span><br />
  <span class="country-name">US</span><br />
Email: <a class="email" href="mailto:msauers@travelin
  librarian.info">
msauers@travelinlibrarian.info </a><br />
Telephone: <span class="tel">999-999-9999</span>
</div>
</div>
```

To those of you familiar with Cascading Style Sheets (CSS), the classes should look a bit familiar. Because all the classes are now there supplying the hCard data, you can also use them to style the presentation of your content using any CSS that's available to you. (The original and completed code can be downloaded from the companion website at http://www.alatechsource.org/techset/semanticweb/.)

Testing

Once you have finished your editing, save your updated staffdirectory.html file and make sure it's available on a publicly accessible server. As it takes Google time to reindex websites, changes in search results will not be automatic (thus, we can't just type our search into the search box of Google and see our work); however, we can use the Rich Snippets testing tool to see if we have formatted the data correctly.

Open a web browser to http://www.google.com/webmasters/tools/richsnippets, and enter the URL of the webpage you've just created. Click "Preview," and cross your fingers.

If you receive the error message "Insufficient data," then something is not formatted correctly; you will need to compare your work against the example. If you are using an existing site that has more content than our staffdirectory .html page, you may need to add more microformatted metadata to pass the test.

If all of your code has been correctly entered, you should see a screen similar to the one in Figure 5.8, which shows our results. In this case, you'll see a sample result of a search for your site, along with a breakdown of all of your hCard data. As you can see, Google now "understands" much of your data. For example, we know that "Sauers" is the family name for Michael and that Robin's postal code is "30602."

From a searcher's point of view, Google's understanding of this data allows for better search results. Instead of just doing a pure keyword match to some of our data, Google now knows what our data means and can therefore more accurately report it back to a searcher.

When something goes wrong in the coding of your hCard data, Google's Rich Snippets tool will give you a warning to help highlight the problem. You will need to fix all problems in order to validate your page, that is, for your page to pass the test. Rich snippets coding is not required for Google to index the page's content, so validation errors are not the end of the line for your content.

Rich Snippets is a valuable tool, especially for libraries, when moving toward offering more services via mobile platforms. Many libraries also provide a Google search engine to search across their websites, and these can be customized to make use of extracted rich snippets, offering a unique experience to users.

Going Mobile

Another advantage of enriching data with rich snippets is that much of the type of information that is semanticized is the same type of data used in many popular mobile devices. Although there are other ways to create mobile applications for calendars and contact info, using vCards for contact information, for example, you are indeed creating portable data. Most web

▶ Figure 5.8: Successful Validation of hCard Data

browsers and mobile devices have plug-ins or add-ins for finding and using vCards. Firefox has Matchbook (https://addons.mozilla.org/en-US/firefox/tag/vcard); BeamMe (http://www.beamme.info/) is a free iPhone app for vCards; and vCardIO (http://code.google.com/p/vcardio/) is a free Android app, to name just a few.

In terms of development, many QR code generators will take a URL, including for sites that have vCards, and turn it into a QR code that can be publicized on the site. You can also add a "download this" vCard by using a free service from Technorati by adding a link on your site (<a href= "http://feeds.technorati.com/contacts/*yourURLhere*">download vCard</a>). You can also host and create your own services, too; truly, the sky's the limit in terms of what you can offer to your mobile users!

Remember, metadata is generally not seen by humans. If you enrich your pages with Google's Rich Snippets, you may not *see* any visible differences, but you should notice that your content is easier to find. Google search results will also display contextual information as well as be more portable—this is how metadata is designed to work. It is designed to help computers talk to each other, to help search engines find and make use of our information, and to harness the power of mobile devices and web tools. Enriching your metadata using Google's Rich Snippets helps make your web content more semantic, especially to Google, and creates data that is portable and readily available to mobile devices. A staff directory marked up with the hCard microformat can be downloaded from your site into cell phones and other mobile devices. Good metadata is crucial to a good search experience. It is often overlooked because it is not a pretty image on a website, but it is a beautiful functionality.

▶ CONTRIBUTE LINKED DATA TO A CIVIL WAR PROJECT

As a final exercise, let's take a look at a project that's going on right now in honor of the sesquicentennial of the U.S. Civil War. Your library may not have the right kind of data to contribute to this particular project, but it is a great example of what can be done when data of a certain type, held by many different libraries and institutions, is semanticized so that it can work as a single, larger data set. To help us illustrate how this project works, we've brought in Jon Voss, Project Manager of the Civil War Data 150 project (http://www.civilwardata150.net/), to walk us through this example.

Go to http://www.alatechsource.org/techset/semanticweb/ to access this figure: The Civil War Data 150 Project

Hundreds of collections of American Civil War data are distributed across the United States in the form of library holdings, museum artifacts, and archival collections. While some of this information is discoverable via the World Wide Web generally, the vast majority can be found only through finding aids on the websites of holding institutions. Civil War Data 150 (CWD150) is a collaborative project to share and connect Civil War–related data across local, state, and federal institutions during the four-year sesquicentennial of the Civil War, beginning in April 2011. The project utilizes Linked Open Data to find and create semantic links among 20 to 30 collections in libraries, archives, and museums and to help increase the discovery and usability of these resources by researchers and the general public alike.

Based on the primary vocabulary of the Civil War, individual item-level holdings are linked to regiments or battles and eventually to individual soldiers. A letter from a soldier can be associated with a regiment, for instance, as can a regimental flag, a regimental history book, muster rolls, and so forth. Battle maps, photographs of battlefields, and the like are associated with battles. Connecting geospatial information, dates, and other linkable data to the regiments and battles exponentially grows the web of interconnected Civil War data, ultimately allowing us to visualize and analyze the Civil War like never before.

A Three-Phase Process

In the three phases of the CWD150 project, five major areas critical to growing Linked Open Data for libraries, archives, and museums are addressed: open licensing of institutional metadata, tools for publishing metadata, utilization of shared vocabularies, tools for utilizing open data sets across the web, and the creation of use cases specific to library, archive, and museum metadata. CWD150 is in the first phase of the project at the time of this writing.

Phase I

The initial phase of the project is to collect raw metadata from participating institutions. This phase focuses on educating institutions about the basics of Linked Open Data, exploring the details of metadata licensing options, and publishing metadata to a central repository.

Step 1: Identify an Appropriate Collection

The best candidates for contributions to CWD150 are data associated with objects that can be ascribed to a Civil War soldier, regiment, or battle. These could be journals, regimental flags, photographs, letters, muster rolls, service records, or pension records. Collections and databases not directly related are welcome as well, although some work may be needed to create the appropriate vocabulary for your specific collection.

Step 2: Export Collection Metadata as a Structured Data File

Once appropriate collections are identified, they can be harvested through various existing protocols (OAI-PMH, Z39.50) or simply submitted in the form of .csv or .xml files (two-dimensional aggregates of metadata). The preferred option is a .csv file with descriptive metadata in columns. Include URLs to the items and images if there are any. If you can identify regiments or battles in the collection holdings, you can create columns especially for these, which will be mapped to a single vocabulary in the next phase.

To see an example of a simple dataset culled from the Library of Congress's Prints and Photographs Division, go to http://www.alatechsource.org/techset/semanticweb/ to access this figure (full .csv file also included): Sample CWD150 Dataset

Step 3: Choose a License for the Metadata

To qualify for this project, an open license must be granted to the metadata (this license does not apply to the underlying assets, such as photographs and journals). The licensing options include the following:

▷ Creative Commons Attribution (CC BY)
▷ Open Data Commons Attribution License (ODC BY)
▷ No Rights Reserved (CC0)
▷ Public Domain Dedication and License (ODC PDDL)
▷ Creative Commons Public Domain Mark (CC PDM)

Metadata that is contributed with a more restrictive license than these might be used for vocabulary alignment but cannot be published as Linked Open Data for the purposes of this project.

Step 4: Publish the Metadata File to CWD150

1. Go to http://www.archive.org/details/civilwardata150.
2. Click "Upload" at the top right of the page and follow the instructions.
3. *Important:* Be sure to use "CWD150" in the keywords.
4. After the file is uploaded, e-mail data@civilwardata150.net to notify the project of your contribution.

An alternative to uploading directly is to e-mail the file to data@civilwar data150.net and specify what license you are applying to the data.

Phase II

The second phase involves "vocabulary alignment" or connecting the disparate data sets to common denominators. In this case, we're starting with Civil War battles and regiments as our key vocabulary. We will utilize tools such as Google Refine (http://code.google.com/p/google-refine/) as well as various scripting tools and algorithms to parse out connections, but we'll also utilize crowdsourcing tools in this phase to gain clarity from human judgment and encourage the public to help make or discover the connections.

The crowdsourcing element provides a unique opportunity for students, enthusiasts, and the general public to interact with primary materials from the Civil War while contributing valuable information to the project. Building off of research from projects such as Old Weather and Ancient Lives from Zooniverse (http://www.zooniverse.org/), we'll introduce simple gaming elements to engage participants in a series of tasks that help forward the project and track individual contributions. By asking "yes" or "no" questions, for instance, we're able to sort photographs into categories that we're unable to ascertain from the metadata and then create separate tasks or games that ask for different inputs, such as placing a photo on a map.

Step 1: Metadata Analysis and Automatic Alignment

The first task is to examine the spreadsheets to see if regiments or battles are referenced in the metadata. If so, various scripting can be done to parse out that data and then reconcile it against the vocabulary of battles and regiments using Google Refine. In the case of the earlier example of Library of Congress metadata, we can see that the 7th NY State Militia is identified, and this will be reconciled and matched with variations of the name in Step 1 or 2.

Step 2: Human Intervention

A number of crowdsourcing tools and data games will be available to ask "yes" or "no" questions, identify regiments or battles, place photos on a map, and geo-rectify maps. These will be accessed through a central website, which will also contain teaching tools and curriculums regarding primary sources related to the Civil War.

Phase III

The third and final phase involves publishing the metadata as Linked Open Data and building visualizations that both aid Civil War historical research and seamlessly demonstrate how previously isolated data sets can be meshed for different purposes. Here, we explore the use of tools for both publishing and consuming Linked Data for academic research.

To view examples of similarly visualized data (although not all specifically related to the Civil War) in the forms of an interactive map, an interactive timeplot, and an interactive timeline, go to http://www.alatechsource.org/techset/semanticweb/ to access these figures: Interactive Map: Civil War Conflict History; Interactive Timeplot: New Legal Permanent Residents in the U.S. (per year) vs. U.S. Population vs. U.S. History; Interactive Timeline: The Kennedy Assassination

Step 1: Serializing Linked Data

Based on the vocabulary alignment of Phase II, item-level collection data will be serialized as RDF triples and made available on the CWD150 website and the Internet Archive. The metadata serialized will include Library of Congress subject headings, National Park Service battles and regiments, and geospatial information.

Step 2: Publishing Linked Data

The open data sets, in RDF, JSON, and .csv formats, will be hosted both on http://civilwardata150.net and http://archive.org. They will also be published to http://freebase.com, where they will be reconciled against existing data about Civil War regiments and battles and where they will be available for access through the open source Acre programming tools.

Although the vocabulary is not yet finalized, let's take a look at our first line of data from our sample data set (Table 5.2) and then compare that to the RDF coding we'd need to add to the data. (The data itself has been reformatted to fit the layout of this book. Refer to the actual data set on the companion website at http://www.alatechsource.org/techset/semanticweb/ for a better display.)

Now, we need to add the RDF code to the appropriate data fields for each of the items in our data set. So, continuing with our first item, we need to reformat it into our agreed upon structure. Thus, we end up with the following result:

▷ **Table 5.2: Sample Data Set**

Field	Value
Callnumber	LOT 4189 [item] [P&P]
DateCreatedPublished	[photographed 1861, printed later]
Medium	1 photographic print
Repository	Library of Congress Prints and Photographs Division, Washington, D.C. 20540 USA
Summary	Soldier, holding bayoneted rifle, standing full-length in front of tent, African-American male seated beside him, and others in tent
Title	7th N.Y. State Militia, Camp Cameron, D.C., 1861
imageURL	http://lcweb2.loc.gov/service/pnp/cph/3c20000/3c26000/3c26500/3c26533r.jpg
pageURL	http://www.loc.gov/pictures/item/00651205
thumbnail	http://www.loc.gov/pictures/static/data/media/006/006512/00651205/00651205/gallery.jpg

```
<rdf:RDF>
  <frbr:Work rdf:about="http://www.loc.gov/pictures/item/
  00651205/">
    <dcterms:title>
      7th N.Y. State Militia, Camp Cameron, D.C., 1861
    </dcterms:title>
    <dcterms:subject
rdf:resource="http://www.perseus.tufts.edu/hopper/text?doc
= Perseus%3Atext%3A2001.05.0146%3Achapter%3D30%3Aregiment%
3DNY7StateMilitia"/>
    <dcterms:subject
rdf:resource="http://www.freebase.com/edit/topic/en/7th_new
_ york_militia"/>
    <dcterms:subject rdf:resource="http://id.loc.gov/
    authorities/names/n97059093"/>
    <xhtml:license rdf:resource="https://creativecommons
    .org/publicdomain/"/>
    <cc:attributionName>Source: Library of Congress</cc:
    attributionName>
  </frbr:Work>
</rdf:RDF>
```

As with the previous Google Rich Snippets project in this chapter, all we're really doing is adding XML markup that describes each of the elements in each of our items. Granted, this adds a lot of verbosity, but with each XML element we add, we give computers the ability to not only read but also understand the context of each and every item within our data set. Once the code has been added, we can proceed to send our data to applications that can start manipulating it.

Step 3: Building Apps

Once the data sets are properly encoded, they then become available for building apps, widgets, and data visualizations through any number of tools. CWD150 will provide customized instructions for using Simile Exhibit to create several visualizations with a specific data set as an example, similar to this tutorial: http://simile-widgets.org/wiki/Getting_Started_with_Exhibit.Apps might explore, for example, casualties throughout the war or specific to certain regiments. They may track regimental movement throughout the war on a map or identify battles with lower or higher casualties.

CWD150 is designed as a working model focused on a specific domain that addresses key issues of utilizing Linked Open Data in collaboration with a broad array of libraries, archives, and museums. Beyond a simple demonstration, the project leverages the engagement of institutional partners, creation of crowdsourcing tools, and new visualizations that will be used for academic research.

►6

MARKETING

- ► **Put Someone in Charge**
- ► **Use Third-Party Services**
- ► **Issue Online Press Releases**

Marketing is an important component of a project that is often overlooked with more technical projects. Yet the success of technical projects often rests on library staff and users. For example, to have images in Flickr to tag and enrich metadata, there needs to be images in Flickr—someone has to take those photos, edit them, upload them, and then create metadata for them.

Sharing the work with those in your organization (and beyond) can not only reduce the work that you have to do but also be the key to growing the project. Getting staff enthused about your project will help promote it to the larger community. Staff who understand and participate in your project may also learn new skills or gain a new understanding of the web or metadata, all of which may help them in their daily work. They may have new ideas or work flows for the project that will save time in the continuing maintenance or content creation.

However, it's not just about what you or your project needs. You also need to demonstrate what the value of participating in the project will be. If you're asking staff to take photos and upload them to Flickr, what is the advantage to the staff? How will this help them in their day-to-day work? How will it fit in with the mission and vision of the library? Getting buy-in is not just important, but critical to successful project planning.

►PUT SOMEONE IN CHARGE

If your library has a PR, marketing, or communications department or officer, make sure to talk to them about your project—from the beginning! It may not be necessary to involve them in the actual hands-on work of the project, but they will be able to help you build energy and momentum before the project even launches. The more they know about your project, the better they can promote it. When the project is ready for launch, they should already have a marketing plan and course of action.

If you don't have a PR or marketing department, then it will be up to you to find someone to take charge of marketing. Identify staff (or even people in the community) who would be interested in the project. Get them involved as soon as you can, and empower them to spread the word for you. Help them understand the value of your project—why it is important and why you are doing it. The value may seem obvious to you (who wouldn't want automatically downloadable content info in their mobile device?), but not everyone may understand how it relates to the library. Which promotional tools you use (see the sidebar for some suggestions) will depend on the scope of the project, the involvement of others, and the guidelines of your library or organization.

Tools for Promotion and Marketing

- ▷ E-mail lists
- ▷ Newsletters/newspapers
- ▷ Flyers
- ▷ Social media (Facebook, Twitter, etc.)
- ▷ Blogs
- ▷ Word of mouth/networking
- ▷ Viral (others share your resources through social media)
- ▷ The library website
- ▷ Contests
- ▷ Ads
- ▷ Press releases
- ▷ Demos and training workshops

▷ USE THIRD-PARTY SERVICES

For many Semantic Web and social search projects, the library website will be the front door of the work. In addition, you can incorporate third-party (hosted elsewhere) services like Flickr. Including content such as a rotating slide show that can be pulled into your website using metadata terms to select only certain images will broaden your outreach. Many third-party services publish content, even images and video, using an RSS feed (which uses harvestable data via the API). RSS feeds provide a wealth of possibilities in terms of harvesting content to embed into your website or even into another website, such as a Facebook page.

If your library has a Facebook page, post information about your project on the page. Facebook Pages have recently added support for iframes, which have been commonly used across the web for a while. An iframe is an inline frame; in other words, it allows you to use some XHTML code to include content from one website into an existing website. Facebook's support of iframes essentially means that your library's page can embed nearly any web content. For example, you can use an iframe to use customized CSS from your website into the page to style it more consistently with your library's website. (However, Facebook's current color scheme is blue and white; this color scheme will wrap around whatever you create and cannot currently be overridden.) Iframes also give you the ability to fold in third-party scripts like a slideshow from Facebook. There are many tutorials on Facebook Pages and iframes. (Facebook has put together some excellent ideas on how to use iframes at http://www.facebook.com/note.php?note_id=501377617203.) Because iframe support was just added to Facebook in 2011, libraries are only beginning to explore all of the possibilities of cross-pollinating content to Facebook using this technology.

Other more general tools can also be used on your website and Facebook page to attract new users. Google's FeedBurner (http://www.feedburner .com/) can be used with sites that publish via RSS. FeedBurner is best for more text-heavy content, such as blogs and Twitter, but it will also work with images and podcasts (video). Flickr offers some great tools for creating embeddable content into a website, including the App Garden (http://www .flickr.com/services/), a place to see and find apps developed by others. Should you become more adventurous and want to build your own Flickr-based products, Flickr has a strong development community (http://www .flickr.com/services/api/).

Regardless of what type of project you do, evaluate your library website to see how your project can be promoted by icons, blog posts, and videos explaining why your project is of value. If your project involves a mobile device or a mobile app, make sure to either point people to the app or embed it in your website.

Consider using QR codes (http://en.wikipedia.org/wiki/QR_code). QR codes are a great way to share information with mobile users. They are not limited to print and are easy to create and embed into a website. QRStuff .com is one of the many free generators on the web. Promoting your projects on your website via third-party services is an important part of the overall project management, ensuring a successful and dynamic project.

▷ ISSUE ONLINE PRESS RELEASES

Not only can your website serve as the home of your projects, but it can be the central hub for all of your PR work, too. Press releases, blog posts, e-mails, newsletters, and so forth can (and should) link back to your website and your project's home base on the web. Promotional writing is not meant to be a procedure or a technical document—it is meant to sell. In a society that is saturated with changing technology and something new around every bend, it is important to explain why your project is relevant. However, stressing the relevance of your project should be brief and, in itself, relevant to the particular target audience. PR work is fun, so let your enthusiasm for your new project shine! The end result will be a more dynamic, useful, and content-rich project that benefits staff and community alike.

7

BEST PRACTICES

▶ **Estimate Project Time**
▶ **Determine Staff Skill Sets**
▶ **Identify Funding Avenues**

Best practices for Semantic and Social Web projects are similar to those for other technology-related projects. Before you pick a project, do a little research. A good place to start is to look at peer libraries and institutions. However, don't limit yourself only to organizations that are doing cutting-edge work. Read practical application books (like THE TECH SET series), blogs, and articles. Connect and network with others who have already done a project similar to yours to get tips and ideas about what works and what doesn't.

▶ ESTIMATE PROJECT TIME

Once you have a project idea, estimating a project timeline will save a whole lot of effort and stress down the road. While your plan doesn't have to be perfect (and it never will be), the more planning you do, the more success-ful the project will be. However, don't overplan to the point where the tech-nology that once was new and exciting is now passé and old hat. You don't want your project timeline to be so rigid that there is no room for change or adaptation. A good project timeline should be flexible, allowing enough space (overestimating everything slightly) so that when problems do arise there is some room to make changes or take time to evaluate.

As mentioned earlier in this book, three general project factors are time, resources (including people), and money. In terms of time, when calculating the amount of time you will have to devote to the project, identify any potential deadlines there may be. Do you need to get your Flickr account up and running in time for a summer reading program? Do you need to launch tagging of the library catalog before an influx of freshmen in the fall? If there is no set deadline, determining the timeline in the project management stage becomes even more critical. Given the rapidly changing nature of technology, all technology projects need some sort of maintenance plan. A launch date should be determined, but, beyond that, ongoing maintenance needs to be part of the timeline, too. A project without target dates and a launch date is bound to drag on. If you discover that your target dates are off or that the launch date is going to be postponed, you can change them. If you are constantly missing dates, figure out why. Does your staff not have enough time to work on the project? Do they need more training? Were your time frames unrealistic?

Staff resources are one of the hardest to determine in terms of time. Staff get pulled off onto other projects or cannot commit the time needed to do the project work for a variety of reasons. Knowing how much time is allotted for a project is helpful, but part of that will depend on how much staff time you have at your disposal. If your project will take approximately 60 hours of work and you have two staff who can work only five hours a week on it, in theory, it will take six weeks to finish the project. If you have three staff who can work ten hours a week, it will take two weeks. Solving the problem of how much time staff can devote to a project is not easy. Sometimes it can mean a change in work flows or workloads, increased training to reduce the amount of time needed to complete a project, outsourcing or hiring consultants, utilizing volunteers or interns, or going beyond the initial project group. Having the buy-in of administration is important for securing adequate time and help.

► DETERMINE STAFF SKILL SETS

Staffs are another factor in having a successful project. Knowing what skills will be needed for a particular project allows you to "shop" for staff with those skills, reaching out to those who will be able to do the work of the project. If your project is heavy on metadata or web development, reach out first to the staff whose jobs require these skills, going through the proper channels of course. Staff with similar expertise may also be of help: technical services, web, or IT staff can all help with semantic or search projects. If your library does not have staff who are able to do this kind of work, reach out to volunteers or to students in a local LIS program who need internships or practicums. Every project will require some kind of training; after all, you are launching something new. The amount of training needed will depend on the complexity of the project as well as what skills staff bring to the table.

Technology support is a big factor in semantic projects. Not only will you have to identify staff who can do the work needed, but you will also need to determine what kind of software, computers, and other hardware (cameras, scanners, etc.) may be needed. Does the project require any special software? Does existing software meet the needs, or will you have to upgrade? Do not forget to check out your server, too; some web projects can take an extraordinary amount of space or tax Internet resources greatly. Your web infrastructure needs to meet the requirements of your project. One way to double-check your technology and web infrastructure is to reach out to your IT staff; if you are putting together a project group, adding an IT person can help smooth the project process.

▶ IDENTIFY FUNDING AVENUES

Your project won't succeed if you can't pay for it. Staff time, electricity, and server space all cost money. Depending on your library, you may be able to identify potential grants from your city, regional or national library organization, or other organizations, such as the Institute of Museum and Library Services, the Bill & Melinda Gates Foundation, or the Mellon Foundation, among others. If you are going to apply for a grant, it may cover a lot of the expenses of the project.

Without additional funding sources, you will have to rely on your library's resources and staff time to do the project. To supplement them, reach out past your library and tap into "free" resources. Reach out to volunteers, interns, and graduate students doing practicums (not only LIS but also computer science, Internet technology, and web development students). Some websites, such as Flickr, Facebook, and Google, have development communities that provide free documentation and/or training. The W3C (http://www.w3.org/) writes documentation, develops standards, and makes recommendations for best practices for all matters web related—all for free. Other library organizations, slideshare.net (a repository where users share presentations), and the open source community offer free services as well.

Computer hardware for free is the hardest of all of the resources to locate. Your organization or city may have a surplus or be willing to give your library a "hand-me-down" that will work for your project. It is also possible that you might be able to upgrade your computer hardware to meet the needs of your particular project; however, that is most likely just a quick and temporary fix to larger technology needs.

Your website's usage and participation statistics, number of website visits, and so forth can be used to measure the success of your project. This is discussed in the next chapter.

▶8

METRICS

- ▶ **Collect Website Statistics**
- ▶ **Employ User Experience and Usability Testing**
- ▶ **Use Other Measures of Success**

The tools you use to measure the success of semantic and social search projects will depend somewhat on the types of project that you undertake, their complexity, and the types of statistics you want to gather. Library website statistics, third-party website statistics (Facebook Pages, YouTube, and Flickr all provide some statistics), user feedback, participation, and social media influence (the amount your content is shared via social media sites) are all viable forms of measuring success.

▶COLLECT WEBSITE STATISTICS

For projects that involve your library's website, you should be able to collect data from the server logs via statistical software or a product such as Urchin (http://www.google.com/urchin/index.html). If your library does not currently collect its own website statistics, you may receive statistics from a larger organization; your campus, consortia, or library system may collect statistics for you. Regardless of who actually collects your statistics, you will need to talk to them about what kinds of statistics you would like to see. If your library does not have direct access to the server logs, you can use one of the free tools out there directly on your website, including Google Analytics (http://www.google.com/analytics/; see Figure 8.1) and JAWStats (http://www.jawstats.com/), which works in conjunction with AWStats (http://awstats.sourceforge.net/).

Third-party websites usually provide their own statistics. Sometimes these are free, such as Facebook Pages statistics, while others offer statistics only as a feature of a paid account, such as Flickr's statistics (http://www.flickr.com/photos/username/stats/). Flickr collects a variety of site statistics from

► Figure 8.1: Google Analytics

measuring popular images to overall statistics. As with any site statistics, what is measured is based on what is collected. With third-party sites you may have little influence over how much data you can collect or even what you can do with that data.

► EMPLOY USER EXPERIENCE AND USABILITY TESTING

Another useful tool for measuring the success of web-based projects is usability testing. Usability testing attempts to find out what users actually do while at your website and how useful the website is to them. Does it meet their basic needs and expectations? Are they able to successfully accomplish tasks at your website? We often think that we know what our users want, but when they actually interact with our websites and products, we find that we are sometimes, maybe even often, wrong. In terms of a specific project, usability testing attempts to determine how users interact with your project. For example, with a Flickr-based metadata project, you would analyze the Flickr statistics in terms of how often and how your patrons interact with your Flickr images. Do they add tags? Do they share images? Do they add comments and/or notes? All can be indicators that your patrons are engaged and using a particular project.

You can also survey, interview, or ask for feedback from your users about a particular project. Offering an incentive to complete the survey or provide feedback will increase the number of respondents and their willingness to contribute. Free survey tools include Google Documents (http://docs.google .com/; use the forms and spreadsheets) and SurveyMonkey (http://www .survey monkey.com/). If your library has a Facebook page, you can either embed survey information into it using an iframe, or you can use an existing survey app available through the apps directory (http://www.facebook .com/apps/directory.php), such as Survey (http://www.facebook.com/ simple.surveys). Other tools to gather information are specifically for projects housed on your library's website. Software that generates heat maps, such as ClickHeat (http://www.labsmedia.com/clickheat/index.html), will actually capture the "hot" and "cold" spots of your website. In other words, you can see exactly where your users interact with your website or project.

▶ USE OTHER MEASURES OF SUCCESS

Other measures of success include how often your content is shared across social media. Statistics gathering across social media sites is still evolving; however, there are a few tools you can use. If you have a Facebook page or account, you can add a like or friend button to your library's website. Facebook Pages also have much more robust statistics than personal pages. If you are a library or organization and want to track your social media statistics in terms of your users, you will need to create a page if you do not already have one.

Another tool to evaluate how often your content is shared across public social media sites, blogged, or mentioned on the web is to create a Google Alert (as we covered in Chapter 5). Google Alerts can be very useful for evaluating the effectiveness of specific web projects, especially if there has been a big marketing approach.

There is also an emerging field of social media metrics that assesses reputation and influence. Several sites, such as Klout (http://www.klout.com/; see Figure 8.2), PeerIndex (http://www.peerindex.com/), and Twitter Grader

▶ Figure 8.2: Klout Analysis

(http://tweet.grader.com/), provide a free analysis of your social media presence. Each differs slightly in terms of which sites and what they evaluate, but, generally, the primary targets are LinkedIn, Facebook, and Twitter, with a focus on how active your community is (how much they interact with your account in social media spaces, how often you are retweeted on Twitter, how often your links are shared on Facebook, how many people are in your network, etc.). As social media continues to grow, social media metrics will become increasingly important, and we will see more services that pull together statistics across a variety of sites. More traditional measures of success include word of mouth. How often do patrons ask about a particular feature or product? Do staff tell users about your project and encourage them to use it?

A final component of determining project success is an internal audit of the project. Did it meet the objectives of the project plan? Why or why not? Is it being used and how? Are some parts of the project being more heavily used than others? If so, what can you determine from your usability testing? Does your design cause issues or barriers to using the project website? If you had to do the project over again, what would you do differently? What would you do the same? Writing up an evaluative summary not only is a good practice but also will help with future projects, too.

▶ 9

DEVELOPING TRENDS

- ▶ **Check Out Open Library**
- ▶ **Explore Linked Open Data**
- ▶ **Consider the Virtual International Authority File**
- ▶ **Investigate OpenCalais**

As the Semantic Web and Social Web continue to evolve, we will see new ways of using data to create more personalized services and products. For libraries we will continue to see our data open up to the larger web community. RDA (the new cataloging standard) and its framework, FRBR, will not only make our library catalogs more semantic in terms of functionality but also make our data more semantic friendly to the larger web community, provided that our data is not siloed.

Traditionally, our databases and data have been locked away—at worst, completely inaccessible to search engines; at best, accessible but with data that is hard for a search engine to interpret. Libraries, vendors, and software developers are already starting to look at RDA and FRBR and discussions about open data. Barriers among data sources—barriers between community-generated metadata through social media sites and structured data like traditional website metadata and barriers among the platforms of mobile, desktop, and web sources—will continue to fall.

As the world moves toward more mobile platforms, we will continue to see the exchange of data from our devices to the web, to our computers, to our cars, and even to our household appliances. Our world will truly become net-worked together in a way that is individual and customizable—all of it driven by the ability of machines to understand each other facilitated by metadata. As for the Semantic Web, we won't suddenly wake up to a Semantic Web; the Semantic Web is just a natural evolution. Google, Microsoft, and Yahoo! have recently paired up to create semantic schemas (http://schema.org/), including schemas for books and other materials that libraries typically collect. So, in the future, we may find our library data for our resources has become so portable that it is readily mapped (converted) to other schemas for a variety of different communities across the Internet and easily portable to a variety of devices we can yet imagine. Cutting-edge Semantic Web projects abound on the web, many of which are very much in development and thus are changing rapidly. A few developing semantic projects of interest to libraries are Open Library, Linked Open Data, the Virtual International Authority File (VIAF), and OpenCalais.

▶ CHECK OUT OPEN LIBRARY

Open Library (http://openlibrary.org/) is a web-based project from the Internet Archive (http://www.internetarchive.org/) and is partially funded by the California State Library. The goal of the Open Library is to create one webpage for every book. To date the project has collected over 20 million records and 1.7 million scanned books from various resources (including library catalogs). Open Library is available to everyone, and anyone can contribute to it (though a free account is required). While Open Library is a giant catalog, it goes beyond just indexing bibliographic data. The beauty of Open Library is that its database (InfoBase) and data structure follow a Semantic Web structure; each part of the record is an object that can be indexed or used (in other words, a lot of potential linking of data, i.e., Linked Data). Searchers can use a robust suite of filters, download books, and also borrow (or buy) books. Open Library is also looking at the future of library catalog data (FRBR, which is the framework that will go around RDA).

Open Library is a semantic project with much potential for the Semantic Web, and it also folds in social functionality (the ability to make lists, for one). Open Library is certainly a potential search tool and resource for those looking for e-books or to expand offerings beyond what is in their library.

▶ EXPLORE LINKED OPEN DATA

The Linked Open Data project (http://data.nytimes.com/) is a project of the *New York Times* to release its own data of authoritative (names, places, etc.) vocabularies for Semantic Web functionalities and projects. These vocabularies are licensed under Creative Commons and can be used under the appropriate terms of use. Not only are these vocabularies available, but creating linked data (relationships and connections) among the various terms is ongoing. In addition to this project, the *New York Times* supports a robust project development site that provides an API tool and other utilities (http://developer.nytimes.com/tools) for working with information and content shared through the *New York Times*. For those interested in developing their own semantic tools or projects, both of these websites are rich resources not only as an existing vocabulary but also in terms of seeing semantic markup in a more understandable format. For example, look at the entry for J&J Snack Food Corporation at http://data.nytimes.com/N8543242210 5120048222.

▶ CONSIDER THE VIRTUAL INTERNATIONAL AUTHORITY FILE

Another vocabulary tool is the Virtual International Authority File (http:// viaf.org/). The VIAF is a project of OCLC in collaboration with several libraries, including the Library of Congress, the Getty Research Institute, and the National Library and Archives of Canada.

The goal of this project is to share author authority records so that all works by a particular author can be indexed under his or her name. Because this database is truly international, it can help bring together different variations of a name and can be a resource for librarians, library users, and anyone searching for author, corporation, or creator information (of a work that is held by a library, of course). The VIAF is still very new, and use of its data is governed by OCLC's usage policies, which do limit is use within the larger Semantic Web community.

▶ INVESTIGATE OPENCALAIS

OpenCalais (http://www.opencalais.com/) is software developed by Reuters to create and share open data, providing not only linking points but also the ability for users of OpenCalais to tag people, places, and events, using standardized vocabularies. OpenCalais can be downloaded and used by anyone (though it must be hosted on your own web server), and the content must be publicly available. It can be used with web content management systems like Drupal, WordPress, OpenPublish, and others, including Marmoset (a script that can be used on traditional webpages), which will actually take OpenCalais-enriched data and ready it for Google Rich Snippets and Yahoo Search Monkey. OpenCalais makes standardizing and enriching web content on an existing website much simpler without a significant need for coding.

In terms of metadata, each of these projects incorporates elements of the Semantic Web without disregarding the social nature of the web. Offering great potential in terms of the Semantic and Social Webs, these projects will undoubtedly continue to grow and become more robust. By the time you read this, there will undoubtedly be a new tool, yet undiscovered as of this time. We will find new inspirations—as well as new tools and resources to help semanticize our data, in addition to finding new ways of searching and indexing data.

Certainly the future will continue to focus on more interchangeable data and more sharing of data, allowing us to customize the web and our world to fit each of us uniquely. This is the beauty of the Semantic Web—machines will finally make our lives easier, eliminating redundant tasks by knowing what we need from them based on the preferences that we determine.

RECOMMENDED READING

▶ BOOKS

Antonious, Grigoris, and Frank van Harmelen. 2008. *A Semantic Web Primer.* 2nd ed. Cambridge, MA: MIT Press.

> This is a good primer to Semantic Web terminologies, structures, and principles, including RDF, XML (syntax, schema, and query), Web Ontology Language (OWL), and logic, using case studies, examples, and a companion website to expand knowledge.

Berkun, Scott. 2008. *Making Things Happen: Mastering Project Management (Theory into Practice).* Sebastopol, CA: O'Reilly.

> Berkun offers commonsense advice and practical tips for facing challenges when leading projects and teams, focusing on both successes and failures.

Berners-Lee, Tim. 2000. *Weaving the Web: The Original Design and Ultimate Destiny of the World Wide Web.* New York: Harper Paperbacks.

> Written by Tim Berners-Lee, "the father" of the World Wide Web, this book encompasses the past, present, and future of the web. It is an excellent resource to frame thinking in terms of web technologies.

Clifton, Brian. 2010. *Advanced Web Metrics with Google Analytics.* 2nd ed. Hoboken, NJ: Sybex.

> This practical guide to using Google Analytics encompasses both introductory and more complex tips for web metrics from implementation to analysis.

Coyle, Karen. 2010. *Library Technology Reports, Understanding the Semantic Web and RDA Vocabularies: Two-Issue Set.* Chicago: ALA TechSource.

> This is a "must read" for libraries explaining how library data fits (and will fit) into the Semantic Web world.

Dowd, Nancy, Mary Evangeliste, and Jonathan Silberman. 2009. *Bite-Sized Marketing: Realistic Solutions for the Over-Worked Librarian.* Chicago: ALA Editions.

The authors provide practical marketing tips and ideas for libraries, including online and guerrilla marketing and the benefits of new technologies over traditional print marketing.

Fensel, Dieter, et al. 2005. *Spinning the Semantic Web: Bringing the World Wide Web to Its Full Potential.* Cambridge, MA: MIT Press.

This is a good overview behind the scenes of the current web—what makes it work (and doesn't) and how the Semantic Web will work differently and more efficiently, using flexible structures and linking data.

Kruk, Sebastian Ryszard, and W.D. McDaniel. 2009. *Semantic Digital Libraries.* New York: Springer.

Using case studies and initiatives, the authors explore the possibilities, challenges, and shortcomings of the Semantic Web in terms of digital library materials.

Lewis, James. 2005. *Project Planning, Scheduling & Control, 4E: A Hands-On Guide to Bringing Projects in on Time and on Budget.* New York: McGraw-Hill.

Guidelines and practical business examples and projects in this book address issues and provide tips for successful project management; additionally, it includes study tips for the Project Management Professional (PMP®) exam.

Pollock, Jeffrey T. 2009. *Semantic Web for Dummies.* Hoboken, NJ: Wiley.

This book is an easy-to-understand primer of the foundations of the Semantic Web.

Russell, Matthew A. 2011. *Mining the Social Web: Analyzing Data from Facebook, Twitter, LinkedIn, and Other Social Media Sites.* Sebastopol, CA: O'Reilly.

Russell provides an overview of how to work with APIs for Facebook, Twitter, LinkedIn, and other sites.

Sauers, Michael P. 2010. *Searching 2.0.* New York: Neal-Schuman.

Searching 2.0 focuses on practical "super-search" strategies for use with blogs, RSS, wikis, Flickr, and the Social Web for librarians and information professionals.

Segaran, Toby, et al. 2009. *Programming the Semantic Web.* Sebastopol, CA: O'Reilly.

Targeted to developers, *Programming the Semantic Web* provides a technical overview of the Semantic Web with a focus on programming needed to build Semantic Web applications.

Smith, Gene. 2008. *Tagging: People-Powered Metadata for the Social Web.* Indianapolis: New Riders Press.

This is a good overview of tagging, its reach beyond traditional metadata, and how tagging relates to the Social Web.

Taylor, Arlene, ed. 2007. *Understanding FRBR: What It Is and How It Will Affect Our Retrieval Tools.* Englewood, CO: Libraries Unlimited.

This is a good overview of FRBR especially as it relates to library catalogs and data, making it an important read for all librarians.

▷ ARTICLES

Berners-Lee, Tim, James Hendler, and Ora Lassila. 2001. "The Semantic Web: A New Form of Web Content That Is Meaningful to Computers Will Unleash a Revolution of New Possibilities." *Scientific American*, May 17. http://www.scientificamerican.com/article.cfm?id=the-semantic-web.

This is an excellent short introduction and overview of the Semantic Web, encompassing ontologies, structure, and more.

Byrne, Gillian, and Lisa Goddard. 2010. "The Strongest Link: Libraries and Linked Data." *D-Lib Magazine* 26, no. 11/12. http://www.dlib.org/dlib/november10/byrne/11byrne.html.

Written with a library perspective, this article focuses on linked data, introducing the basic concepts of linked data and how it will work. Most important, it discusses the benefits of using linked data, challenges for libraries, and changes that need to happen in order to move library data forward.

Chatfield, Carl. 2011. "A Short Course in Project Management." Microsoft. Accessed November 28. http://office.microsoft.com/en-us/project/HA102354821033.aspx.

Here's a good overview and introduction to project management, covering the fundamentals of time, cost, and scope.

Danowski, Patrick. 2010. "Step One: Blow up the Silo!—Open Bibliographic Data, the First Step Towards Linked Open Data." IFLA Conference Session 149. http://www.ifla.org/files/hq/papers/ifla76/149-danowski-en.pdf.

This paper explores the often overlooked (yet crucial) topic of licensing, especially as it relates to library data for use in Semantic Web projects.

Dunsire, Gordon, and Mirna Willer. 2010. "Initiatives to Make Standard Library Metadata Models and Structures Available to the Semantic Web." IFLA Conference Session 149. http://www.ifla.org/files/hq/papers/ifla76/149-dunsire-en.pdf.

Metadata initiatives utilizing library standard formats and structures such as FRBR, FRAD, and ISBD accessible to the Semantic Web are reviewed.

Heery, Rachel, and Harry Wagner. 2002. "A Metadata Registry for the Semantic Web." *D-Lib Magazine* 8, no. 5. http://www.dlib.org/dlib/may02/wagner/05wagner.html.

This scholarly and technical article explores metadata registries and their roles on the web utilizing Dublin Core Metadata Initiatives.

Hillmann, Diane, et al. 2010. "RDA Vocabularies: Process, Outcome, Use." *D-Lib Magazine* 16, no. 1/2. http://dlib.org/dlib/january10/hillmann/01hillmann.html.

This article covers the RDA standard and its parallel effort to build Semantic Web–enabled vocabularies, which can be used within libraries and as a link with nonMARC metadata systems.

Scott, David Meerman. 2008. "New Rules of Viral Marketing." David Meerman Scott. Accessed November 28, 2011. http://www.davidmeermanscott.com/documents/ Viral_Marketing.pdf.

> This is a good overview of viral marketing and social media as they relate to business.

Sheikhnajdy, Zahara, Mehran Mohsenzadeh, and Mashalab Abbasi Dezfuli. 2011. "Improving Semantic Schema Integration." *World of Computer Science and Information Technology* 1, no. 5. http://www.wcsit.org/pub/2011/june/Improving%20Semantic% 20Schema%20Integration.pdf.

> This in-depth article takes a technical look at metadata mapping in terms of how it works in the Semantic Web with ontologies and protocols.

Vatant, Bernard. 2010. "Porting Library Vocabularies to the Semantic Web, and Back. A Win–Win Round Trip." IFLA Conference Session 149. http://www.ifla.org/files/ hq/papers/ifla76/149-vatant-en.pdf.

> Using the Telplus project as a case study, this paper provides guidelines for making library metadata vocabularies more useful and efficient to Semantic Web functionalities; additionally, it reviews Semantic Web tools in terms of vocabulary management.

▶ WEB RESOURCES

LibSuccess.org. 2011. *Marketing* (wiki). Accessed October 28. http://www.libsuccess .org/index.php?title=Marketing.

> This wiki is devoted to library marketing best practices, providing resources, case studies, marketing plans, and recommended readings for marketing in libraries.

LinkedData.org. 2011. "Linked Data—Connect Distributed Data across the Web." Accessed July 27. http://www.linkeddata.org/.

> This is a resource portal for linked data, including tutorials, glossary, research, and data sets that can be used for research, education, or projects.

Miller, Paul. 2011. *The Semantic Web.* ZDNet. Accessed July 2. http://www.zdnet.com/ blog/semantic-web.

> This chronological list provides brief descriptions of blog topics from ZdNet on the Semantic Web that encompass a variety of concepts, such as Linked Data.

SemanticWeb.org. 2011. *The Semantic Web* (wiki.). Accessed July 27. http://semantic web.org/wiki/Main_Page.

> This wiki and portal for the Semantic Web community includes tools, ontologies, and links to Semantic Web–related events.

W3C. 2011. "Image Annotation on the Semantic Web." W3C Incubator Group Report. Accessed July 27. http://www.w3.org/2005/Incubator/mmsem/XGR-image- annotation/.

This technical report focuses on semantic metadata for images, including guidelines for Semantic Web–based image annotation using case studies as examples.

———. 2011. "Semantic Web Activity." Accessed July 2. http://www.w3.org/2001/sw/.

Home to the W3C's Semantic Web activity, this site lists the current projects.

Wikipedia. 2011. "Semantic Web." June 26. http://en.wikipedia.org/wiki/Semantic_Web.

This definition, overview, and history of the Semantic Web includes examples of current Semantic Web projects and an extensive reference list.

———. 2011. "Social Search." Accessed July 2. http://en.wikipedia.org/wiki/Social_search.

This definition and overview of social search includes examples of current social search projects.

———. 2011. "Social Web." Accessed July 2. http://en.wikipedia.org/wiki/Social_web.

This definition, overview, and history of the Social Web includes examples of current Social Web projects and an extensive reference list.

INDEX

ABOUT THE AUTHORS

Robin M. Fay is Head of Database Maintenance for the University of Georgia Libraries. A frequent guest lecturer and teacher, her areas of interest are metadata, semantic web, and social media. You can find her at http://robin fay.net/.

Michael P. Sauers is Technology Innovation Librarian at the Nebraska Library Commission. This is his eleventh book.

CPSIA information can be obtained at www.ICGtesting.com
Printed in the USA
BVOW080810130812

297727BV00005B/1/P